The Cucumber Field Guide

The Cucumber Field Guide

Practical Examples for Automated Software Testing

Steven Hunt

Additional content as well as the source code for build tools used to generate the final printed edition of this work are available on GitHub:

https://github.com/stevenmhunt/cucumber-field-guide

The information provided within this book is for general informational purposes only. While we try to keep the information up-to-date and correct, there are no representations or warranties, express or implied, about the completeness, accuracy, reliability, suitability, or availability with respect to the information, products, services, or related graphics contained in this book for any purpose. Any use of the methods described within this book are the author's personal thoughts. They are not intended to be a definitive set of instructions. You may discover there are other methods and materials to accomplish the same end result.

Edited by Michele Elder

First Edition: July 2024

ISBN: 979-8-3302-3595-7

Visit my website at https://stevenhunt.me/book

Contents

Chapter 10: Building a Test Framework — 107

Chapter 11: Interacting with Systems — 133

Preface

Every journey begins with a single step. This is true for both implementing automated testing and for writing books about automated testing, so here we go. After spending the past decade working on test automation with the Cucumber testing tool in both development and QA teams, I've decided to collect all of my knowledge, experience, thoughts, and opinions into a guide for people interested in learning more about test automation and what is possible with it.

The goal of this book is to provide practical advice for developers and testers who want to use Cucumber and the Gherkin language to test their applications so they can improve the quality of their software—and also have some fun in the process. Whether you're new to test automation or seeking guidance for how to improve the quality of your existing tests, you have come to the right place.

The ideas in this book come from a variety of sources including my own personal experiences working on large software projects. I've heard it said that "failure is another word for experience",[1] so it won't surprise you to learn that many of the "pro tips" and "pitfalls" mentioned in the book come from my own ~~failures~~ experiences and how I learned from them. One of the struggles of writing software is that you can never reach perfection: technology is always changing, the customer's requirements are always changing, and developers are learning and changing. So remember that perfection is a moving target. My hope is that by reading this book, you'll be able to avoid some of the challenges I've encountered over the years and get a little closer to the "perfect test suite."

Assumptions

Before starting work on software projects or writing tests, it's always a good idea to identify and document your assumptions. Taking the time to do this at the beginning of a project can result in new realizations about requirements, limitations, and unanswered questions, saving everyone on your team an enormous amount of time and frustration. Since this is a book about testing, I would think it's appropriate for me to do the same before you begin to flip through the pages. I've made assumptions both conscious and unconscious that are woven into the words I write, the code I type, and the thoughts and actions I engage in every day. I believe that the more each of us becomes aware of these assumptions and learns how to articulate them to others, the better our communication with other people is going to be, the less that unnecessary conflicts will arise, and the happier and more productive we will all be. With all of that in mind, let's discuss some of these assumptions in more detail.

---

[1] A quote by George Lucas regarding creative endeavors.

Who Should Read This Book

If you're reading this book hoping to learn new ways to grow, harvest, prepare, and eat delicious green vegetables, you're going to feel let down. As much as I personally like to make salads and other sorts of dishes with cucumbers, I am not prepared to write an entire book on the subject. However, in the spirit of writing a book with "cucumber" in the title, I will include my classic "quick pickle" recipe in the **Afterword** if anyone is interested. I usually make it with red onions, but it works just as well with some cucumber slices, or both! Instead, if you're looking for a practical, hands-on technical guide about software test automation loaded with ideas, recommendations, and sometimes my opinions about utilizing Cucumber and Gherkin (the software), then you're in luck. Alternatively, if you are expecting idealism surrounding test methodology, or perhaps a more theoretical approach, you may also find yourself less than satisfied with the contents of this book.

If you're new to programming or automated testing, I recommend doing some additional reading elsewhere before going any further here, as this book is meant to be a quick reference guide for developers and testers who feel comfortable with basic software development principles and tools.

Testing Approach

Speaking of opinions about testing, this book is focused on integration and end-to-end testing. I will discuss unit testing to some extent, but in my experience, Cucumber is best suited for testing further up the Testing Pyramid, so that will be the focus of most examples. In my opinion, there are many wonderful unit testing frameworks out there and I recommend that you focus your efforts with behavior-driven development (or BDD) at a higher level of abstraction than "units" of code. While it is certainly possible to use Cucumber as a unit testing framework, I would not personally recommend doing so.

About the Book

There are also assumptions that I have made about how you will make use of the information provided in this book. I've organized the ideas presented here into sections that you can reference in the same way you would flip through recipes in a cookbook. As you read through these pages, keep in mind that recipes in general are a starting point and not a panacea, and that what satisfies the needs of one software project does not necessarily apply to others. Ultimately it is up to you to take the ideas presented here and incorporate them into what it is you're doing. I'm simply here to help you consider some new approaches that will perhaps lead you to new and novel solutions for your testing challenges.

That said, this book is intended as a practical guide, so you won't find detailed information on testing methodology here as there are plenty of other books out there that cover that subject in more detail, such as *The Cucumber Book, BDD in Action,* or *Specification by Example.* As alluded to earlier, this book is not idealistic or purist in its approach, so there may be those of you out there who don't like or agree with some examples presented here. Much like a cookbook, if a recipe you find here sounds unsavory to you, simply move on to another one that seems more palatable. I have found that most software developers and testers who have been in the industry for more than a few years have strong opinions about methodologies and processes, so I am certainly not anticipating that you're always going to agree with me.

Throughout the book, I will be providing clear and concise definitions as new terminology is introduced and will be keeping the use of those terms as consistent and unambiguous as possible in order to improve your experience. The practice of maintaining a ubiquitous language during the course of a software project is meant to minimize miscommunication and reduce any friction and frustration that may hamper progress, so I will be following this practice as well.

The book is organized into sections that focus on a particular recommendation or set of related recommendations. Returning to the cookbook analogy for a minute, if you like your food less salty or really enjoy putting cayenne on everything, then by all means tweak and adjust these recipes as desired. While I personally use CucumberJS and sometimes SpecFlow, I have included information on using Cucumber across a range of languages. I am not advocating for a specific programming environment, so use the tool that makes sense for your team and your application. I generally recommend that you write your step definitions in the same language as your software project's code in order to facilitate code re-use and allow better collaboration between QA and developers if you have separate teams. For this book I have chosen Java, JavaScript, and Ruby, as these languages represent a wide range of programming paradigms and styles, all three are fully supported by the official Cucumber project, and the majority of the other language-specific integrations look at least somewhat similar to one or more of them.

About the Author

Hi, I'm Steven. I've been programming since I was in the 7th grade and started interning in my high school's IT department at 16 years old. Since then, I've worked on everything from NASA mainframes to VoIP start-ups, enterprise-scale shipping management, and commercial building security systems. I started in desktop support and server administration, and then spent a lot of my career in a development role. I've also worked in DevOps and QA, where I focused on designing and writing infrastructure and tools to support test automation using Cucumber. When I'm not writing code or talking about software, you'll find me snow skiing, playing piano or guitar, or spending time with my wife and kids.

Acknowledgments

I would like to take this opportunity to acknowledge some special people who have helped me both personally and professionally over the years. I'd like to thank Lou Zulli for opening up the world of IT and software development to me back when I was in high school. Getting two years of experience under my belt before leaving for college opened up a lot of unique opportunities for me, and I am very thankful. I would also like to thank Brandon Binkley, who told me all about BDD and Cucumber back in 2013 and got me interested in test automation. I'd also like to acknowledge Jose Rodriguez, Shannon McRae, Stewart Moon, and Victor Baziuk for taking a chance with Cucumber and helping me to build the most expansive Cucumber test suite I've ever been involved with. Many of the "pitfalls" and "warnings" in this book come from our shared experience on that project, so their contributions to this endeavor are much appreciated.

Finally, a special thanks to my wife Alice for being a loving and supportive partner always and throughout the process of writing this book.

Chapter 1: Introduction to Automation

At one time, software was validated the same way that any other product was tested—by hand. Considering that the primary reason people and companies use software to begin with is to automate repetitive tasks, it makes a lot of sense to automate the testing of that software. While I don't believe that automation can fully replace manual testing, having robust and well-maintained automated tests can improve the quality of your applications while also making your team more efficient, productive, and happy.

1.1 Why Automate Testing?

While manual testing can provide value in certain cases, the sheer size and complexity of modern applications requires some level of automation to properly validate functionality if products of quality are to be delivered to customers within a reasonable time frame. That being said, one of the primary reasons to automate your testing is to actually allow yourself to do more manual testing but with an exploratory focus. I am a supporter of letting computers do what they do best (boring and repetitive tasks) in order to free up humans to do what it is that we do best (identify patterns, make judgments, explore, etc.). Automated testing doesn't replace manual testing, so instead we should be using both techniques to improve the quality of software, which is the ultimate goal of any QA effort.

Many years ago, I worked on a software project that involved a third-party vendor converting our legacy mainframe code into C#. I was in charge of reviewing their delivered builds and tracking bugs, and we had several people on the team dedicated to manual testing. Every week or two, the vendor would send over the latest build, I'd install it onto our servers, and then the testing team would spend the next four or five days running through their manual test procedures. Afterward, we'd collect the results of those manual tests and send a report back to the vendor in order for them to make changes. This process went on for months and was extremely stressful for everyone on the team, especially because there was significant pressure from our government customer to deliver a final product quickly. Even worse, sometimes the latest build from the vendor would be less usable than the previous one. If we had created automated tests written to perform at least a surface-level check of the vendor's builds, a lot of time and stress could have been avoided. Computers don't get tired, and they don't experience emotional stress (except perhaps for Google's AI chatbot[2]), so leveraging automation to handle those aspects of the validation process is ideal for meeting customer delivery dates while keeping the people on your team happy.

---

[2]https://time.com/6186990/google-ai-bot-sentient-lamda/

Every time the source code of your application changes, any previous test results become invalid, especially if (as in the previous example) some or all of the components are outside of your team's control. Considering that the vast majority of applications are built on top of frameworks and libraries that we casually download from the internet with NPM, Maven, gem, pip, etc., most of the actual code being executed as part of a modern application is no longer within our control or the control of a single well-known vendor such as Oracle or Microsoft. This can lead to unexpected bugs or even security vulnerabilities such as CVE-2021-44228[3] or the NPM colors attack[4] and can cause significant impacts to your software.

To respond to these challenges, it is more important than ever to have test automation in place that can allow you to quickly assess if the behavior of your application has changed. Considering the worth of your team's time and mental health, investing in test automation will yield more value than repeatedly testing software manually and then starting from scratch every time there's a change to your application. If your application is small, doesn't integrate with any other systems, and never changes, then automation may not make sense for you. For all other cases, which includes almost all modern software applications, pursuing test automation is a worthwhile endeavor.

Once you have built some automated tests for your application, those tests can then become part of a larger infrastructure collectively referred to as continuous integration and continuous delivery or CI/CD. The more often you run your tests and can begin to depend on them, the more confidence you will gain regarding your tests as well as in the behavior of your entire application. For more detailed information on CI/CD, skip ahead to **Chapter 2**.

1.2 Opportunity Cost

Test automation is an investment, and like any other type of investment there is an upfront cost. At the beginning of your project which is incorporating test automation, the investment will be considerable until you've accumulated a sufficient collection of reusable test steps. You can expect to be spending 50% of total effort on automation for every work item in the first several weeks of development. But as you build up your library of reusable test steps, the amount of effort required for writing new tests will drop significantly. If you made good design choices at the beginning, you will be able to quickly write new automated tests for your software project with little to no coding required. Throughout this book, we will be reviewing strategies and examples on how to accomplish this.

---

[3] https://nvd.nist.gov/vuln/detail/CVE-2021-44228
[4] https://news.ycombinator.com/item?id=29877745

If you work on many similar and closely related software projects, it may be possible for you to reuse your steps across multiple projects, assuming you choose to design your steps with that in mind. The more time and effort you invest up front into your automation architecture, the more value you receive from it in return over time.

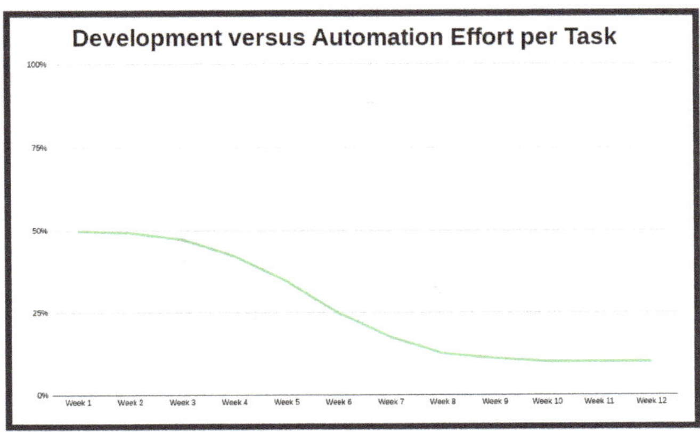

Figure 1: Development versus automation effort per work item.

1.3 Measurable Goals

When planning a significant development effort such as implementing and maintaining automated testing, it is important to consider what your team's goals are. In general, the primary objective of any software QA team is to ensure that software of the highest quality is being delivered to customers within a reasonable amount of time. When customers receive software products riddled with defects that impact their productivity, the reputation and future viability of your product is in peril. That said, it is difficult to prioritize your team's testing efforts without first determining what the desired outcome is. For example, your product may be subject to industry-specific legal compliance requirements, so automating this required testing would be a sensible goal. Other target goals include reducing the number of defects, reducing production outages, or reducing the amount of scripted manual testing.

When considering your goals, remember that every time a piece of software is changed, the previous test results for that software are no longer valid. Also consider that tracking defects and where they originate from is helpful for measuring progress and ultimately improving the quality of software.

1.4 The Testing Pyramid

This wouldn't be a book about testing without the Testing Pyramid.

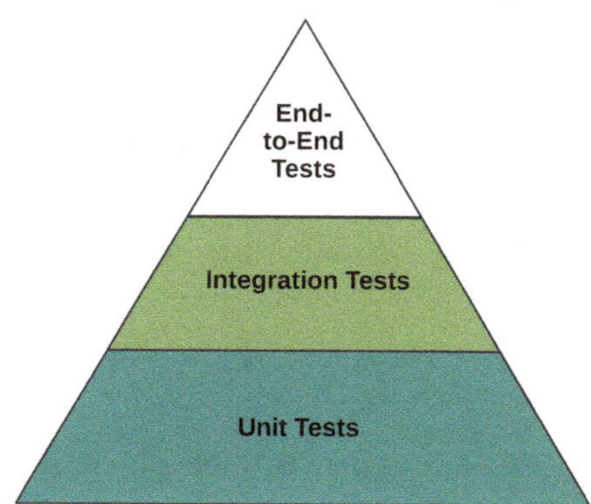

Figure 2: The Testing Pyramid.

There are a lot of variations of this model in books and on the internet. Some of them have four or five layers, or sometimes it's rendered in 3D, so it's actually a pyramid instead of just a triangle. In any case, the intent of this model is to provide a visual reference for what types of tests you should be writing and how much emphasis you should be putting on each of those types. Essentially it says that you should have unit tests for covering all of your software components, you should have a significant amount of testing the integration between components such as your service layer, and finally, some but not all of your testing should be focused on testing your entire application (end-to-end) such as UI testing. However, in my opinion, having a few outstanding tests is much better than 100% code coverage with poor unit testing that creates a false sense of security.

This diagram makes a lot of assumptions by drawing lines between what unit testing, integration testing, and end-to-end testing are. Unfortunately, reality is not quite that simple. For example, while the difference between service testing and UI testing would seem straightforward, there are some specific types of services such as BFFs that have testing characteristics of both. We'll talk more about BFFs in **Chapter 2**.

In an effort to eliminate the ambiguity, some versions of this model have done away with well-defined sections and instead use a gradient where the farther up the pyramid you go the more integration between components is involved in the tests. Unit tests have no integration, integration tests have some amount of integration, and end-to-end tests have full integration with your application's various components and systems.

Chapter 2: Concepts

Before installing and running Cucumber, let's take some time to review core concepts that you'll want to have a solid understanding of before continuing.

2.1 Cucumber versus Gherkin

You may be asking yourself, "What is Cucumber, what is Gherkin, and what is the difference?" Cucumber is the name of the software tool that is used to execute your tests, as opposed to Gherkin, which is the language that you will use to write your tests. Cucumber is able to parse and execute Gherkin in order to determine whether your tests are passing or failing. For more information about Cucumber and Gherkin, skip ahead to **Chapter 3**.

2.2 Ubiquitous Language

An activity worth doing throughout the life of any project is explicitly defining terminology within your team in order to avoid communication confusion. Every project has "jargon" that describes business objects and processes, and taking the time to clearly and unambiguously define those terms is important for the continued success of your project. Eric Evans first coined the term ubiquitous language to describe this concept in his book *Domain-Driven Design* which I highly recommend. I am a firm believer in having a one-to-one relationship between terminology and what is actually being discussed: If your team is using two or three different words to describe the same concept or is using a single term in an ambiguous way, it's going to cause confusion and, eventually, mistakes in your project.

2.3 Test-Driven Development

The most concise and terse description of TDD is "red, green, refactor." Practitioners of TDD write a unit test before implementing code knowing that it will fail without the implementation, hence *red*. Somehow, if the test passes, theoretically no coding is required. Then the functionality is coded as quickly as possible (this is agile, after all) and once the test passes, it is now *green*. Then the code gets cleaned up in the "refactor" step if needed. For more information, refer to the **Further Reading** section.

🏅 **Pro Tip:** If a large portion of your application's logic is contained in database queries, consider using an ORM to abstract your queries and then use an in-memory SQLite database to run your component-level tests. It gives you the power of integration testing with the speed and consistency of unit testing but without spending all day building mocks. For more information, refer to **Chapter 11**.

2.4 Behavior-Driven Development

I have always enjoyed this particular term because on the surface it sounds very simple and self-explanatory: writing tests from the perspective of the end user and focusing the content of those tests on the behaviors the end users are engaging in sounds relatively straightforward and obvious. However, the more you unpack this concept and attempt to make the jump from concept to implementation, the more it becomes clear that you're going to need some new tools to help with this. That's where Cucumber comes in. For more information about BDD, refer to the **Further Reading** section.

2.5 Specification by Example

By choosing to use Cucumber and Gherkin, you are buying into the idea of BDD and specification by example where instead of writing tests as code, you write them as human-readable sentences that also happen to be executable by the computer. This allows you to focus your test cases on more practical scenarios that an end user might experience while using your application, and keeps you from writing esoteric or confusing tests. It also enables these executable specifications to act as a form of documentation for your application. For more information about specification by example, consider reading *Specification by Example* and refer to **Further Reading**.

2.6 Continuous Integration

A common reason for automating software testing is to facilitate continuous integration where you automatically build, deploy, and test your application in your development environment every time the code is changed. CI ensures that your tests will run frequently, and if they do fail, someone will actually notice. For more information about CI and build servers, refer to **Chapter 3** and **Chapter 9**.

2.7 Continuous Delivery

If you already have a fully automated build pipeline where you can build, deploy, and test your application, the next logical step is to automatically promote your application to test or production whenever code changes have been completed and tested. This automatic promotion is referred to as continuous delivery, and together, CI and CD are referred to as CI/CD. In order to implement CI/CD, you must have a clear understanding of the build process, the test coverage, and how your application works within the environment it runs in. In organizations that have successfully implemented this ability, their teams can deploy code changes to production in a matter of hours instead of waiting weeks or months.

2.8 DevOps

DevOps (development operations) is the integration of software development infrastructure (such as source control and CI/CD) with IT operations infrastructure (such as systems monitoring, servers, and databases) while applying automation and agile methodology practices across both development and operations. While not directly related to Cucumber, the use of these tools in a modern development team will typically be within the context of DevOps and CI/CD processes, so it is important to understand how Cucumber and BDD can add value to teams that are implementing these practices. For more information, refer to **Chapter 9**.

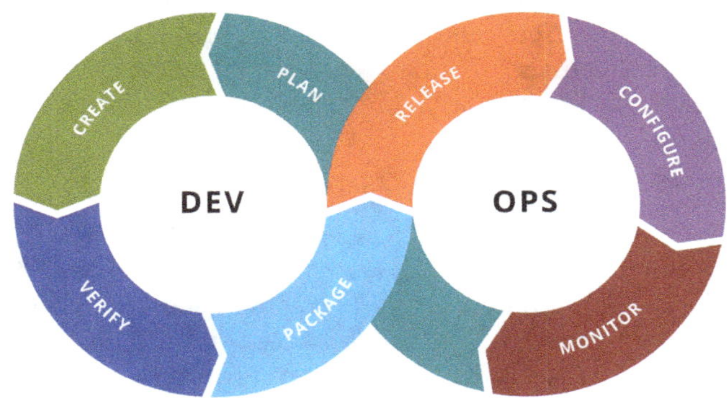

Figure 3: A visual representation of the DevOps workflow[5]

2.9 Testing Pyramid Revisited

The next topic to discuss is where Cucumber fits into the Testing Pyramid. Is it the one and only testing tool you should use? I am a firm believer in choosing the right tool for a given task and even Cucumber is not the right tool for testing in all cases. While it is possible to use Cucumber to perform unit testing, in practice I have found that unit testing is more effective when using a library where you write code directly instead of using abstractions such as Gherkin. One of the advantages of using Gherkin is that you can write tests while separating yourself from the "how it works" of writing code. The power of that really shines when writing tests from a user's perspective, which typically means working at higher layers of abstraction such as testing the UI, BFFs, or service APIs. Depending on the complexity of your application, using Cucumber for component testing may also be a viable option.

---

[5]Kharnagy, CC BY-SA 4.0 https://creativecommons.org/licenses/by-sa/4.0, via Wikimedia Commons

If your application is small enough that you can run significant portions of it using mocks while testing user behavior, then component testing is feasible. However, if your application has a lot of smaller components that integrate together to create the final product, then your pyramid may be "heavier" on the top than the diagram would suggest. Every software project is different, so you must make an evaluation on what is appropriate for yours. What's important is that you write more tests with lower amounts of integration and fewer tests with higher amounts of integration so that the majority of your testing is fast and not flaky and brittle.

⚠ **Caution:** Do not ignore flaky tests. When test results no longer reflect the viability of your application, your team will start to ignore the tests and develop bad habits like rerunning builds without changes or even promoting code with failures present. Fixing tests that fail inconsistently will help maintain trust in your test suite and improve the quality of your application.

2.10 Microservice Architecture

Many modern applications are built using microservice architecture, where the backend components consist of many small (or micro) services. With this style of application becoming more commonplace, a greater emphasis on integration testing is required for software test automation since there are more points of failure arising from the integration of components than in more traditional monolithic application architectures. When integrating tests with modern cloud-based web applications, consider focusing your Cucumber test cases on the service layer, with some testing to cover the UI while having robust and effective unit testing for each component.

💡 **Key Terms:**

> **Microservice** - A software architecture in which the service layer of your application consists of many small services that can intercommunicate. This approach is particularly useful in cloud-based applications since it allows each component of the application to scale separately based on resource demands.

> **Backend-for-Frontend (BFF)** - A type of service in microservice architecture that provides endpoints for a frontend such as a web UI. It allows the UI to interact with a single service and forwards requests to the microservice(s).

There may also be additional considerations that need to be made for different types of microservices such as BFFs, which often contain little to no business logic and simply forward HTTP calls to other microservices. Instead of writing duplicate tests, consider testing your BFFs as part of integration testing so that functional testing can focus on the underlying microservices.

Chapter 3: Tools

Writing good software requires effective tools. Without them, implementing a project of any size or complexity would prove unnecessarily difficult. If your tools are interfering with your ability to work instead of helping you perform a task, find some different tools. There are also different tools for different jobs, so it is imperative that you pick the right tool for the right job in your software project.

3.1 Test Runners

In order to execute your automated tests, you need a test runner. This is a piece of software that scans your project for tests, performs some sort of parsing, and then executes the specific tests that you told it to run. In most cases, the programming language-specific Cucumber tool is the test runner, with the notable exception of SpecFlow for .NET, which is actually a code generator that can target existing .NET test runners such as NUnit, XUnit, and MSTest. A test runner will also expose various configuration options for running your tests, such as fail fast, running tests in parallel, the order in which tests are run, and so forth.

Key Terms:

Code Generator - A software tool that can automatically generate source code as part of its operation. Code generators are particularly common in the C# or .NET ecosystem with examples including the interactive form editors in Visual Studio, Entity Framework model first, and SpecFlow, which converts Gherkin feature files into C# code for the target test runner.

Fail Fast - A testing approach where you stop running tests as soon as a test fails instead of finishing the rest of the tests first, which provides a more rapid response (hence "fast") to CI/CD tools. The downside of this approach is that you'll lose information from any additional failures that may have occurred, so you will encounter those additional test failures one at a time in future test runs instead of all at once.

When choosing which test runner to use, start by looking at the application(s) you're testing. If you can find a Cucumber test runner in the same programming language as your application, that will be ideal especially if you want to incorporate portions of your application's code into your tests. This approach can also improve communication between development and QA teams since they'll be speaking the same language.

3.2 Gherkin

Regardless of which variant of Cucumber you choose, you will use Gherkin
to define tests. Gherkin is a Domain-Specific Language (DSL) that is used to
create human-readable software tests by describing the expected behaviors
of your application. When combined with Cucumber, Gherkin feature files
can be executed as automated software tests.

</> Example #1: A Gherkin Feature File

```
@all-scenarios-will-have-this-tag
Feature: Customers can sign in to the online store.
    I can type whatever I want here, this is for humans.

@scenario-specific-tag @some @more @tags
Scenario: The user logs in and types in the chat box.
    Given the user navigates to the home page
    And the user "test user 1" logs in
    When the user types the following into the chat box:
    """

    This is a long string that may have more
    than one line of text in it...
    """
    Then the chat box should contain text
    And the following fields should be visible on the screen:
    | name   | value |
    | field1 | val1  |
    | field2 | val2  |
    | field3 | val3  |

# you can write comments like this...

  @ruletag
  Rule: Scenarios can be organized into rules

    Scenario: A scenario within a rule
      Given the user navigates to the home page
      When the user "test user 1" logs in
      Then the user should be logged in


@another-tag
Scenario Outline: The user does not log in successfully
    Given the user navigates to the home page
    When the user "<invalid user>" logs in
    Then the user should not be logged in
Examples:
| invalid user |
|  bad user 1  |
|  bad user 2  |
|  bad user 3  |
```

One of the goals of Gherkin is to allow people who aren't programmers to
be able to read and make sense of tests, thus enabling more people within
an organization to understand and validate the expected behavior of your
applications.

Domain-Specific Language (DSL) - A programming language designed for a specific purpose or to solve a specific set of problems, as opposed to a general-purpose language such as C++, Java, etc.

Feature - A set of functionality in your application. Example: "Customers can sign in to the online store."

Scenario - A specific test example that consists of one or more steps, that can be used to validate a feature.

Rule - A grouping of scenarios within a feature.

Scenario Outline - A set of scenarios that use the same steps, but with different parameter values. Gherkin allows for easily adding new test cases to an existing scenario outline, so you don't have to rewrite (or even worse, copy/paste!) repeating scenarios.

Step Definition - A mapping between a human-readable Gherkin step in a scenario and a piece of code that can execute the step. Steps can also contain parameters for reusability.

Scenario Tags - Marks a scenario with a tag so that it can be categorized and targeted for test runs.

Data Table - A table of data that can be passed to a step.

For more information about the functionality supported by Gherkin, refer to **Chapter 7**.

3.2.1 Step Definitions

The magic of Cucumber is that you can produce a document that looks like a set of directions for a human to follow, but it's also runnable by a computer. In order for Cucumber to execute your scenarios, it has to have a map between the human-readable sentences of the steps and some source code that can actually accomplish the task described in the step. This mapping is provided by step definitions.

Without step definitions implemented in some given programming language, Gherkin would simply be a text format for writing manual test procedures. While some form of Cucumber is available in the majority of popular programming languages, this book focuses on three of those languages: Ruby, because it's the original Cucumber step definition language and it represents the dynamically typed indentation-based languages; Java, because CucumberJVM is a very popular implementation of Cucumber and it represents the statically typed object-oriented languages (e.g., SpecFlow in C# is somewhat similar looking); and finally JavaScript, because it represents dynamically typed languages with a functional style and because it runs in both a browser and the terminal. Let's take a look at a step definition in each language and see how they compare:

</> Example #2: A Simple Step Definition

◇ Ruby

Examples in Ruby will be given for Cucumber 8.

```ruby
Given('the user performs some sort of action') do
    # do something...
end
```

▣ Java

Examples for Java will be given for CucumberJVM 7 using an annotation.

```java
import io.cucumber.java.en.Given;

public class MySteps {
    @Given("the user performs some sort of action")
    public void the_user_performs_some_sort_of_action() {
        // do something...
    }
}
```

▤ JavaScript

Examples in JavaScript will be given for CucumberJS 10.

```javascript
const { Given } = require('@cucumber/cucumber');

Given('the user does something', function() {
    // do something...
});
```

🏅 **Pro Tip:** You can use some of the examples from the book with CucumberJS 2 - 6 by changing `require('@cucumber/cucumber')` to `require('cucumber')`.

While all three of these examples appear somewhat different, you can see that they are all effectively performing the same function: they each define a mapping between a step in Gherkin and the code that can execute that step. In this case, I'm using simple strings to define the steps, which works in very simple cases, but for more advanced and reusable step definitions you'll want to define parameters.

3.3 Text Editors

While it is possible to write feature files in any text editor, a more advanced
editor with specific support for Gherkin is recommended. One such IDE is
Visual Studio Code by Microsoft, which has multiple extensions for Cucumber and Gherkin support. Another popular IDE is IntelliJ by JetBrains[6]
which also has support for Gherkin and Cucumber. If you're using C#, the
SpecFlow extension for Visual Studio[7] will install all the required editor
tools.

3.3.1 Microsoft Visual Studio Code

Visual Studio Code needs some prep work before you can start writing tests.

Recommended Extensions

- **Cucumber** by Cucumber[8]
    - The official extension for Cucumber and Gherkin.
- **Cucumber (Gherkin) Full Support** by Alexander Krechik[9]
    - Provides syntax highlighting and auto-complete.
    - Supports automatic document formatting.
- **Snippets and Syntax Highlight for Gherkin** by Euclidity[10]
    - Provides syntax highlight support.
    - Adds snippets and templates for writing tests faster.
- **GitLens** by GitKraken[11]
    - Adds a lot of integrations for `git` directly into Visual Studio
      Code, including inline `git blame`.
- **REST Client** by Huachao Mao[12]
    - A lightweight HTTP client that allows for working directly with
      HTTP requests and responses via text file.

3.3.2 JetBrains IntelliJ

To install plugins, press `Ctrl + Alt + S` and click *Plugins*.

In order to use Cucumber and Gherkin, the following plugins are required:

- **Gherkin**
- Ruby (RubyMine): **Cucumber**
- Java (IntelliJ): **Cucumber for Java**
- JavaScript (WebStorm): **Cucumber.js**

---

[6] IntelliJ IDEA for Java, WebStorm for JavaScript, RubyMine for Ruby

[7] Visual Studio Community, Professional, or Enterprise editions

[8] https://marketplace.visualstudio.com/items?itemName=CucumberOpen.cucumber-official

[9] https://marketplace.visualstudio.com/items?itemName=alexkrechik.cucumberautocomplete

[10] https://marketplace.visualstudio.com/items?itemName=stevejpurves.cucumber

[11] https://marketplace.visualstudio.com/items?itemName=eamodio.gitlens

[12] https://marketplace.visualstudio.com/items?itemName=humao.rest-client

🏅 **Pro Tip:** If you use CucumberJS 2 or later and your auto-complete tool only works with CucumberJS 1, you can use the following workaround in your step definitions:

📜 **JavaScript**

```javascript
function stepLibraryFactory() {
    this.Given('some step', function () { /* ... */ });
    // other step definitions...
}

// allows the IDE tools to "see" the steps.
module.exports = stepLibraryFactory;

// registers the step definitions with CucumberJS.
stepLibraryFactory.call(require('@cucumber/cucumber'));
```

In CucumberJS 1, the program recursively scans the `./features` directory for `.js` files and then loads those files by calling `require()`. It then imports anything that was exported from each of those `.js` files. With the newer versions of CucumberJS, step definitions are registered with the library directly, hence the need for a workaround.

3.4 Build Servers

There are many build servers available for implementing continuous integration such as Jenkins,[13] GitLab,[14] GitHub Actions[15] (used to automatically generate the PDF of this very book!), and TeamCity,[16] just to name a few.

In order to trigger builds, you configure the build server to receive a signal (usually a webhook) from your source control system such as git whenever a change is made to your application, and then it runs a series of steps that you define for your build process. It could be anything from a simple shell script to a fully programmable pipeline or workflow depending on the product you're using. Typically, the build will run some sort of compile or linting step followed by unit tests, a deployment, and finally your higher-level tests. If any part of this process fails, the build server will notify your team and the build will be marked as failed. You can even require that your build passes before allowing a feature branch to be merged into a main branch, allowing your tests to enforce the requirements of your application automatically.

For a complete example of implementing a CI/CD pipeline in Jenkins, refer to **Chapter 9**.

---

[13] https://www.jenkins.io/
[14] https://docs.gitlab.com/ee/ci/
[15] https://github.com/features/actions
[16] https://www.jetbrains.com/teamcity/

Chapter 4 - Planning and Design

While your test suite will grow and change organically as your application grows, it is important to design a proper foundation for your tests before beginning development.

4.1 Gherkin Overview

4.1.1 Overview of Test Automation

Regardless of whether you are performing unit testing, end-to-end testing, or anything in between, automated tests typically consist of three parts:

1) **Arrange:** Set up the conditions for the test.
2) **Act:** Perform an action that needs to be tested.
3) **Assert:** Validate the state of the application.

In Gherkin, these steps are equivalent to Given, When, and Then respectively. Using this pattern consistently in your tests will keep your scenarios organized and help maintain the quality of your test suite.

4.1.2 Gherkin Capabilities

Let's take a moment to review the capabilities of Gherkin:

- **Structured Syntax:** Gherkin uses a structured syntax based on keywords like Given, When, Then, And, and But.
- **Scenario Outlines:** Gherkin supports scenario outlines, allowing you to write a scenario template with placeholders for parameters.
- **Data Tables:** Gherkin allows the use of data tables to provide structured input or expected output for a step.
- **Docstrings:** Gherkin supports docstrings, which are used to include large multiline text blocks as arguments for steps.
- **Backgrounds:** The `Background` keyword allows you to define steps that are common to all scenarios within a feature.
- **Comments:** Gherkin allows for comments using the # symbol.
- **Tags:** Gherkin has scenario tags denoted by the @ symbol, which allow you to categorize and filter scenarios.
- **Rules:** A new feature in Gherkin is the ability to group scenarios within a feature using rules. You can also use `Background` within rules instead of at the feature level.
- **Languages:** Gherkin has support for English and other languages.

The purpose of Gherkin is to create human-readable automated tests. This helps in fostering collaboration among stakeholders, including nontechnical team members. Gherkin and Cucumber act as a bridge between business stakeholders and development teams by providing a common language for discussing and defining software behavior. Its simplicity and expressiveness make it a powerful tool for implementing behavior-driven development.

</> **Example #3:** A Gherkin Feature File

```gherkin
# language: en
# the language comment at the top is used to set the language (default is "en")

@feature-tag
Feature: This is where you describe a feature of the application being tested.
    I can type whatever I want here, this is for humans.

# use a Background to run these steps before any scenario in the feature file.
Background:
    Given the user navigates to the home page

@scenario-tag
Scenario: The user logs in and types in the chat box.
    Scenarios (or Examples) represent an individual test case.

    # steps can accept inline parameters:
    When the user "test user 1" logs in

    # steps can accept docstring parameters:
    And the user types the following into the chat box:
    """
    This is a long string that may have more
    than one line of text in it...
    """

    # steps can accept data table parameters:
    Then the chat box should contain text
    And the following fields should be visible on the screen:
    | name   | value |
    | field1 | val1  |
    | field2 | val2  |

  @rule-tag
  Rule: Scenarios can be organized into rules
    This allows more organization within a feature file.

    Background:
      When the user "test user 1" logs in

    Scenario: A scenario within a rule
      Then the user should be logged in

@scenario-outline-tag
Scenario Outline: The user does not log in successfully
    A scenario outline is a repeatable scenario with parameters.
    It can accept multiple examples via the Examples statement(s) below.

    When the user "<invalid user>" logs in
    Then the user should not be logged in

Examples:
| invalid user |
| bad user 1   |

@scenario-example-tag
Examples:
| invalid user |
| bad user 2   |
```

4.2 Designing Steps

When writing scenarios in Gherkin there are three types of steps that you will use: Given, When, and Then. Each type of step has a different role within a scenario, so it's important that you design and develop steps with these different roles in mind. Ideally, you want the steps in your test suite to be interchangeable and extensible, which means all of your steps need to operate under a common set of assumptions.

4.2.1 Guidelines

Here are some common guidelines for steps regardless of whether they are Given, When, or Then steps.

- Keep a step's wording concise and avoid long steps.
- Decide whether to write steps in first-person (such as "I") or third-person (such as "the user")
- Avoid words like "and"; a step should accomplish a single task.
- Steps that use docstrings or data tables should end with a colon.
- Try to maintain a consistent "look and feel" between steps so that they make sense together in various combinations.
- Use ubiquitous language so terminology used in steps is consistent.
- The wording of steps should focus on what action is being performed instead of "how" it is being performed.
- Avoid negatives except as required for assertions (e.g., should not exist, should not equal, etc.)

🏅 **Pro Tip:** If you have both UI and API testing in your test suite, consider defining a convention for how to differentiate between which steps work at which level of integration. For more information, refer to **11.7**.

4.2.2 Given Steps

When an automated test starts to run, the first task to perform is configuring the initial state of the test in order to ensure that the software is in an expected state before performing the actions being tested. In Cucumber, it is the role of Given steps to perform these tasks. In practice, this means that Given steps change the state of the test but do not perform assertions. Write Given steps in the present tense, not past tense. Also, a Given step should clearly describe the expected state of the test. Here are some examples:

```
Given the customer has cleared their shopping cart

Given the user has selected a flight from "ROC" to "ATL"

Given the user's account has a balance of $0
```

4.2.3 When Steps

Once the initial state of your test has been configured, it's time to perform an action that you would like to test. In Cucumber, we use When steps for performing an action we are testing. The When step itself should not perform any validation on the state of the test after performing the action and should ideally not cause a scenario to fail. For some QA teams there is no functional difference between Given or When tests, while in others a Given step will fail or skip a scenario if an exception occurs. For example:

```
When the diner requests a window seat during the reservation

When the user updates their profile picture

When the customer proceeds to checkout
```

4.2.4 Then Steps

After performing an action that you wish to test, the scenario will need to check the state of the test to determine whether it passes or fails. In Cucumber, the Then steps perform the validation after an action is completed. These steps should not alter the state of the test in any way, but simply assert whether the application is in the expected state. Here are some additional guidelines for Then steps:

- Always include the word "should" in your Then steps to differentiate assertion steps from Given or When steps that perform the action specified in the step name.

- The last step(s) in a scenario should be a Then step. Otherwise, what assertions are you performing in your test?

Here are some examples:

```
Then the user's itinerary should include a 10% discount

Then the confirmation page should display the total price

Then the user's profile should show the updated picture
```

🏅 **Pro Tip:** As your step definitions become more numerous and complex, consider writing unit tests for your steps where you mock a simple application in order to validate that your step definitions are working as expected. Otherwise, you may end up in a situation where it is unclear which is broken, your steps or your application.

4.3 Standardizing Steps

When you start implementing test automation, there will be an investment
of time to write step definitions so that the scenarios required to test the
functionality can be executed. As development of an application moves
forward, the amount of time spent writing step definitions should decrease,
and new tests should be able to utilize the existing suite of steps that have
already been implemented. The underlying assumption here is that the step
definitions are built to be reusable and extensible. In order to design and
build step definitions with these qualities, planning is required.

4.3.1 Create a Standards Document

Just like with source code, it is important to have standards for how steps are
formatted to establish a consistent aesthetic to your tests so that your team
can be more efficient and comfortable when reading through or developing
tests. Consider some ideas from the recommended standards for writing
steps presented in this book and also incorporate your own rules based on
what makes sense for your team. Once you've identified the standard you
want to apply to your test suite, write it down and make sure your team
is aware of the standards. When new step definitions are committed to
source control, review the new steps against your standards to make sure
they are compliant. Remember: once step definitions are available for use,
it's difficult to remove them.

Pro Tip: Consider using a tool such as gherkin-lint[17] to automatically
enforce style rules within your Gherkin feature files. This tool is written in
`NodeJS` but is for Gherkin feature files, so your backend language of choice
does not matter. To get started, run `npm install gherkin-lint`.

4.3.2 Have a Planning Meeting

"Can't this just be an email?" you ask, but in this case it must be an actual
meeting or even more than one if needed. If your team works in the same
physical space at least some of the time, you should have this meeting in
person. Otherwise, a remote meeting is acceptable; however, you will want
to make use of a collaboration tool that your team is comfortable with as
the meeting will need to be very dynamic and interactive.

Stakeholders   One of the advantages of Gherkin and Cucumber is that
they allow people who aren't comfortable with code to read through and
review the tests. So while it's obvious that developers and testers should
be part of this meeting, you should also invite project managers, business
analysts, product owners, or anyone else who has a stake in the requirements
of the software, whether they are technical or not.

---

[17]https://github.com/gherkin-lint/gherkin-lint

Assumptions   Before having a planning meeting to decide upon an initial design of step definitions, it is important that you have at least some grasp on the requirements of your application. If that is not the case, consider utilizing Impact Mapping or a Pirate Canvas to better understand your application's requirements before proceeding. For more information on these topics, consider reading *BDD in Action* and refer to **Further Reading**.

Preparation   Before the meeting, you will want to take some time to write up a set of "proposed steps." This is not a coding exercise; this is purely an attempt at designing some steps that could be used for testing your application. You will also want to write some example scenarios utilizing these steps. Again, we're not doing anything outside Gherkin yet; writing step definition code can come later. Finally, prepare one or more "requirements" that can be used to build a scenario and save them for the meeting.

At the Meeting   The agenda for the meeting should be as follows:

1) Provide an overview about Cucumber
2) Review the proposed step definitions
3) Demonstrate a simple scenario example using your proposed steps
4) Present a "requirement" to the team and collaboratively write a scenario

The goal of the meeting is to get the team to think through how to write a test for your application and work together on writing some tests, so it's important to encourage discussion and collaboration here. You want people attending the meeting to bring up difficult situations, unexpected challenges, and new things that you hadn't thought of yet. You want to perform a trial of your proposed steps and identify potential issues or missing steps before doing any development work.

If you are having the meeting in person, print out several copies of the steps and cut out each step as a strip, along with some blank pieces of paper, so you can write new steps or change existing ones in real time with a pen. Alternatively, if you are having the meeting remotely, choose a collaboration tool to create a similar experience as described above in the in-person meeting, perhaps using a Trello board[18] or whiteboard feature of your favorite video conferencing tool. If there are a lot of people at the meeting, consider breaking up into smaller groups and working on one requirement each, and then review the results at the end of the meeting.

---

[18]https://trello.com/

4.4 Determining Test Types

Before writing tests for your application, you'll need to decide what types of tests are going to be written and when in your software development process these different types of tests are going to be run. Let's look at some commonly used types of tests:

4.4.1 Test Types

Unit Testing Automated testing of individual functions or "units" of code. These tests should use mocks for I/O.

Component Testing Automated testing of whole components or systems. These tests should have minimal to no integration and use mocks for I/O.

Service Testing Automated testing of service APIs such as HTTP-based RESTful services. These tests are integration tests.

UI Testing Automated testing of the UI. If you are mocking the service layer, a UI test could be integration testing. But in many cases UI tests are considered a form of end-to-end testing.

Smoke Testing A type of end-to-end testing that performs a sanity check of an application. These tests should run quickly in order to determine viability, so use a curated subset of your tests.

🏅 **Pro Tip:** Consider building your smoke tests to be safe to run in your production instance, so you can use them for performing health checks. You can also use this approach for running canary builds. For more information, refer to **Chapter 9**.

Performance Testing A type of end-to-end testing that measures the performance of a system under load.

Functional Testing Automated testing that validates a requirement specific to the application being tested.

Non-functional Testing Automated testing that evaluates performance, reliability, or some other test criteria that is not directly part of an application's functional requirements.

Acceptance Testing Automated testing that validates both functional and non-functional aspects of an application in order to determine whether the application is ready to be "accepted" by users.

Regression Testing Automated testing that runs after a software change to validate whether a build has "regressed" or not. Any type of functional or non-functional test from any level of the Testing Pyramid can be run for regression testing.

4.4.2 Relationships Between Test Types

With so many types of testing to consider and with so much overlap between test types, it can be difficult to decide how the different test types relate to each other. Let's take a look at the relationship between test types and how they relate to the Testing Pyramid.

≣ **Table:** Relationships between different test types:

Type	Functional	Regression	Smoke	Acceptance	Level
Unit	yes	yes	no	no	unit
Component	yes	yes	no	no	unit
Service	yes	yes	yes	no	int
UI	yes	yes	yes	yes	e2e[19]
Performance	no	yes	yes	yes	e2e

4.4.3 Choosing Regression, Smoke, and Acceptance Tests

Based on the table above, you can see that these three testing types cut across the other types of testing within your test suite. This means that as tests are being added to your application, you must consider whether these new tests are candidates for one or more of these test types.

Regression Testing: Since these tests are run every time the source code of your application is changed, they need to be reasonably fast but cover a wide range of functionality to ensure your builds are working as expected. Consider using the Testing Pyramid for inspiration and run all of your unit testing, some of your integration testing, and a little of your end-to-end testing on every build. This mix will require frequent tweaking until the right balance between performance and code quality is met.

Smoke Testing: This type of test should be run frequently as part of monitoring and health checking. A select subset of end-to-end testing should be marked for inclusion into smoke testing that does not have persistent side effects on the state of your application so that they can be safely rerun.

Acceptance Testing: These are the final tests run to ensure that your application is ready for customers. If you are using CI/CD, you can assume that many automated tests have already been run on this release candidate build before reaching the point of being considered ready for customers, so skip those tests if appropriate.

---

[19] UI testing may or may not be end-to-end in nature.

4.5 Defining Special Scenario Tags

While more of a planning activity than a development effort, taking the time to intentionally define a standard set of scenario tags for your test suite will help to keep your tests organized and ultimately enable you to target specific subsets of tests within a CI/CD pipeline.

4.5.1 Common Scenario Tags

Every application will have its own list of tags and metadata you will want to associate with a test. Here are some common examples for your consideration.

- `@smoke`: High-level smoke tests that cover critical functionality and verify basic system integrity. You can target these tests when you need to quickly evaluate whether your application build is viable.
- `@functional`: Functional tests that validate specific functional requirements of the application. Adding tags with specific work item numbers on each scenario is also highly recommended.
- `@integration`: Tests that focus on the integration of multiple components or modules. Consider also adding tags that indicate which components of the application are being integrated, so you can target all affected integration points when a specific component in your application changes.
- `@ui`: Tests that validate an application's user interface. These tests often require additional server resources and tend to be more unstable and time-consuming than other types of tests, so categorizing them separately can help your team decide when and where is appropriate to run these tests.
- `@wip`: Indicates that a scenario is "work in progress" and should not be run by CI/CD. This is useful for committing scenarios into source control before they affect the pass/fail status of a build.
- `@unstable`: Indicates that a scenario was implemented but later became unstable and should not be run by CI/CD. You can use this tag to "off-ramp" a troublesome scenario and work on it without holding up CI/CD, assuming your team has made the determination that this is allowable in the context of the affected test. The QA team should be aware how many of these scenarios exist and must constantly be working to reduce the number of these scenarios to zero.

The scenario tags in Gherkin aren't simply static metadata to be used by people reading the tests; they can be leveraged for targeting specific subsets of tests as well as for reporting. In a future example, we'll even see how to use scenario tags with hooks to allow for powerful new testing capabilities.

</> Example #4: Scenarios with various Scenario Tags

```
@functional @APP-STORY-112
Scenario: functional test for story STORY-112
# ...

@functional @APP-STORY-113 @wip
Scenario: function test (wip) for story STORY-113
# ...

@ui @APP-STORY-112
Scenario: UI test for story STORY-112
# ...

@integration @component1 @component2
Scenario: integration test for component1 and component2
# ...

@functional @APP-STORY-115 @unstable
Scenario: function test for story STORY-113, marked as unstable
# ...
```

🏅 **Pro Tip:** You can add scenario tags to all scenarios in a feature file by adding them above the `Feature: ...` line at the top. Since your functional, integration, and UI tests should be in separate files, you can use one of those scenario tags at the top of the file, and then you don't need to repeat them for every scenario.

4.5.2 Gherkin Tag Expressions

Gherkin tag expressions[20] provide a powerful way to filter scenarios based on their tags. The expressions are common across all implementations of Cucumber and allow you to define complex filtering conditions. For example, the expression `@smoke and @ui` would select scenarios tagged with both `@smoke` and `@ui`. Here is a scenario that would be returned by the previous expression example:

```
@smoke @ui
Scenario: The user logs in successfully
    Given the user navigates to the home page
    When the user "user1" logs in
    Then the user is signed in
```

🏅 **Pro Tip:** You can change the behavior of your step definitions based on the scenario tags associated with the currently running scenario. For more information, refer to **Chapter 6**.

---

[20] https://github.com/cucumber/tag-expressions

Chapter 5: Installation

Before we start writing scenarios, we need to get a starter project configured with the required software packages. Follow the directions below for
configuring your development environment in Ruby, Java, and JavaScript.

5.1 Installing Cucumber (Ruby)

Difficulty: ★ ☆ ☆ Easy

Required Software: Ruby,[21] Gem,[22] Rake[23]

Pro Tip: Rails[24] generators can be used to configure Cucumber by
opening a terminal and running `rails generate cucumber:install` if you
are using Rails for your project. For this book, the directions are provided
for installing Cucumber without Rails.

If you are creating a new project:

1) Create an empty directory for your test project.

2) Create a file `rakefile`:

```ruby
require 'rubygems'
require 'cucumber'
require 'cucumber/rake/task'

Cucumber::Rake::Task.new(:features) do |t|
    t.cucumber_opts = ['--format pretty']
end
```

Setup Directions:

1) Open a terminal and run `gem install cucumber`

2) Open a terminal and run `cucumber --init`

Running Tests: Open a terminal and run `rake features`

Additional Guidelines:

- feature files are placed in `./features`
- Step definitions are placed in `./features/step_definitions`
- Hooks are placed in `./features/support`

---

[21] https://www.ruby-lang.org/en/
[22] https://rubygems.org/
[23] https://github.com/ruby/rake
[24] https://rubyonrails.org/

5.2 Installing CucumberJVM (Java)

Difficulty: ⭐ ⭐ ☆ Medium

Required Software: Java JDK,[25] Maven*[26]

*In this book, examples use Maven; however, you can also use Gradle.[27]

If you are creating a new project, use the Cucumber Java Skeleton project.[28] You will also need to change the `@SelectClasspathResource` annotation value to `/features` and create the directory as shown in steps 4 and 5.

Setup Directions for JUnit 5:

1) Ensure your project is targeting Java 1.8 or higher.

2) Add the following to `/project/dependencies` in `./pom.xml`:

```xml
<dependency>
    <groupId>io.cucumber</groupId>
    <artifactId>cucumber-java</artifactId>
    <scope>test</scope>
</dependency>
<dependency>
    <groupId>io.cucumber</groupId>
    <artifactId>cucumber-junit-platform-engine</artifactId>
    <scope>test</scope>
</dependency>
<dependency>
    <groupId>org.junit.platform</groupId>
    <artifactId>junit-platform-suite</artifactId>
    <scope>test</scope>
</dependency>
<dependency>
    <groupId>org.junit.jupiter</groupId>
    <artifactId>junit-jupiter</artifactId>
    <scope>test</scope>
</dependency>
```

3) Add to `/project/dependencyManagement/dependencies`:

```xml
<dependency>
    <groupId>org.junit</groupId>
    <artifactId>junit-bom</artifactId>
    <version>5.10.1</version>
    <type>pom</type>
    <scope>import</scope>
</dependency>
<dependency>
    <groupId>io.cucumber</groupId>
    <artifactId>cucumber-bom</artifactId>
    <version>7.15.0</version>
    <type>pom</type>
    <scope>import</scope>
</dependency>
```

---

[25] https://www.oracle.com/java/technologies/downloads/
[26] https://maven.apache.org/
[27] https://cucumber.io/docs/tools/java/#gradle
[28] https://github.com/cucumber/cucumber-java-skeleton

Given the following:

`<Pkg Name>`: The name of the package, e.g., `com.example.project1`

`<Pkg Path>`: The package directory path, e.g., `com/example/project1`

4) Create a file `./src/test/java/<Pkg Path>/RunCucumberTest.java`:

```java
package com.example.project1;

import org.junit.platform.suite.api.ConfigurationParameter;
import org.junit.platform.suite.api.IncludeEngines;
import org.junit.platform.suite.api.SelectClasspathResource;
import org.junit.platform.suite.api.Suite;

import static io.cucumber.junit.platform.engine.Constants.PLUGIN_PROPERTY_NAME;
import static io.cucumber.junit.platform.engine.Constants.GLUE_PROPERTY_NAME;

@Suite
@IncludeEngines("cucumber")
@SelectClasspathResource("/features")
@ConfigurationParameter(key = PLUGIN_PROPERTY_NAME, value = "pretty")
@ConfigurationParameter(key = GLUE_PROPERTY_NAME, value = "<Pkg Name>")
public class RunCucumberTest {
}
```

5) Create a directory `./src/test/resources/features`.

Setup Directions for JUnit 4:

 **Pro Tip:** It is recommended that you use JUnit 5 if possible.

1) Update the `./pom.xml` file to add `cucumber-java` and `cucumber-junit` packages.

2) Create a file `./src/test/java/<Pkg Path>/RunCucumberTest.java`:

```java
package com.example.project1;

import io.cucumber.junit.Cucumber;
import io.cucumber.junit.CucumberOptions;
import org.junit.runner.RunWith;

@RunWith(Cucumber.class)
@CucumberOptions(features = "src/test/resources", plugin = { "pretty" })
public class RunCucumberTest {
}
```

For additional information, refer to Cucumber documentation.[29]

Running Tests: Open a terminal and run `mvn test`.

Additional Guidelines:

- feature files are placed in `./src/test/resources/features`
- Step definitions are placed in `./src/test/java/<Pkg Path>`
- Hooks are placed in `./src/test/java/<Pkg Path>`

---

[29]https://cucumber.io/docs/cucumber/api/?lang=java#junit-4

5.3 Installing CucumberJS (JavaScript)

Difficulty: ★ ☆ ☆ Easy

Required Software: NodeJS and NPM (LTS release)[30]

If you are creating a new project:

1) Create an empty directory for your test project.

2) Open a terminal and run `npm init`. Fill out the prompts.

Setup Directions:

1) In a terminal, run `npm install @cucumber/cucumber --save-dev`

2) In the `./package.json` file, update the "test" script command to: "cucumber-js"

🏅 **Pro Tip:** On Windows, the default shell for NPM run scripts will be `cmd` even if you initiate your command from `bash`. You can change the default shell for NPM run scripts as follows (assuming 64 bit Git for Windows with default installation paths): `npm config set script-shell "C:\\Program Files\\git\\bin\\bash.exe"`

3) Create the following directories:

- `./features`
- `./features/step_definitions`
- `./features/support`

Running Tests: Open a terminal and run `npm test`

Additional Guidelines:

- feature files are placed in `./features`
- Step definitions are placed in `./features/step_definitions`
- Hooks are placed in `./features/support`

---

[30]https://nodejs.org

Chapter 6 - Developing Step Definitions

Now that our development tools are installed and configured, it's time to start writing step definitions.

6.1 Basic Step Definitions

Creating step definitions in Cucumber is relatively straightforward. First you'll create a code file in your step definitions directory (refer to **Chapter 5** for specific paths for your language-specific Cucumber) and then you can start writing your steps. When Cucumber runs, it will scan for your step definitions and look for a matching step when running scenarios.

</> Example #5: Logging Into an Application

Let's get started with a simple example that you'll see in most Gherkin test suites: having a user log in to your application. We will assume that your application has a `performLogin` function that can be called.

```
Feature: The user logs in
    As a user
    I need to be able to login to the application
    in order to perform my required tasks

Scenario: The user logs in successfully
    Given the user logs in
    # when the user performs some action...
    # then some sort of assertion is executed...
```

◇ Ruby

Creating step definitions is relatively simple in Ruby.

```ruby
require './src/session'

Given('the user logs in') do
    performLogin
end
```

▣ Java

There are two ways to define step definitions with CucumberJVM. Most examples in this book will use a Java annotation such as `@Given`.

```java
import io.cucumber.java.en.Given;
import com.product.app.Session;

public class MySteps {
    @Given("the user logs in")
    public void the_user_logs_in(String user) {
        Session.performLogin();
    }
}
```

You can also define your step definitions as Java lambda expressions.

```java
import io.cucumber.java8.En;
import com.product.app.Session;

public class MySteps implements En {
    public MySteps() {
        Given("the user logs in", (String user) -> Session.performLogin());
    }
}
```

⚠️ **Caution:** The Java 8 version of CucumberJVM is being considered for deprecation[31] by the Cucumber community.

 JavaScript

Creating step definitions with CucumberJS is also relatively straightforward.

```javascript
const { Given } = require('@cucumber/cucumber');
const { performLogin } = require('../../src/session');

Given('the user logs in', async function() {
    await performLogin();
});
```

🛑 **Anti-pattern:** Complicated Step Definition Functions

A step definition function should only contain enough code to perform an assertion or call code elsewhere that implements the desired functionality. You should never write more than a few lines of code in your step definition function, and avoid calling other step definition functions from within it. We'll be looking into assertions more in depth in the next section.

⚠️ **Pitfall:** Ambiguous Step Definitions

Scenarios will fail to run if Cucumber cannot find a matching step definition for a given step in your scenario, or if there is more than one matching step definition. Avoid writing step definitions that are too similar to each other, especially if using Regular Expression matching. Otherwise, your step definitions may be considered ambiguous at runtime by Cucumber.

🏅 **Pro Tip:** Align the language implementation of Cucumber with the language your application is written in to allow for directly using components from the application through your step definitions. In the previous example, the `performLogin()` function that was being called was part of the application itself. Service and UI tests may not interact directly with the application's code in this way; however, there may still be value in allowing your tests to have access to your application's code.

---

[31] https://github.com/cucumber/cucumber-jvm/issues/2174

6.2 Step Definition Statuses

When Cucumber executes a step, there are several possible outcomes:

undefined - A matching step was not found.

failed - More than one matching step was found, or there was an error while running the step.

passed - The step ran without error.

pending - The step was marked as *pending*.

skipped - The step was marked as *skipped*.

If Cucumber is outputting to the screen using the default formatter, it will automatically print step definition stubs for undefined step definitions. These stubs will automatically mark the step as pending until you add your own implementation code.

6.2.1 Pending Scenarios

If you want to add step definitions to your code when they are not yet ready to be run by Cucumber, you can mark them as **pending**.

</> **Example #6:** Marking Step Definitions as Pending

◇ **Ruby**

```ruby
Given('this step is not ready to use') do
    pending
end
```

▣ **Java**

```java
import io.cucumber.java.en.Given;

public class MySteps {
    @Given("this step is not ready to use")
    public void given_some_step_is_not_ready_to_use() {
        throw new io.cucumber.java.PendingException();
    }
}
```

▤ **JavaScript**

```javascript
const { Given } = require('@cucumber/cucumber');

Given('this step is not ready to use', function () {
    return 'pending';
});
```

6.2.2 Skipping Scenarios

For some QA teams, there is no functional difference between Given or When tests, while for others, a Given step will fail or skip a scenario if an exception occurs. It is possible to evaluate preconditions of the test and then skip the test instead of failing it. Here is an example of conditionally skipping a scenario:

</> Example #7: Conditionally Skipping Scenarios

◆ Ruby

```ruby
Given('this given step is going to experience an error') do
    skip_this_scenario
end
```

▣ Java

For JUnit 4:

```java
import io.cucumber.java.en.Given;
import org.junit.Assume;

public class MySteps {
    @Given("this given step is going to experience an error")
    public void given_this_step_is_going_to_experience_an_error() {
        Assume.assumeTrue(false);
    }
}
```

For JUnit 5:

```java
import io.cucumber.java.en.Given;
import org.junit.jupiter.api.Assumptions;

public class MySteps {
    @Given("this given step is going to experience an error")
    public void given_this_step_is_going_to_experience_an_error() {
        Assumptions.assumeTrue(false);
    }
}
```

▤ JavaScript

```javascript
const { Given } = require('@cucumber/cucumber');

Given('this given step is going to experience an error', function () {
    return 'skipped';
});
```

🏅 **Pro Tip:** You can use scenario tags or your test configuration to control whether to perform validation in a Given step. You can also conditionally skip scenarios from a `Before` hook. For more information on these topics, refer to **Chapter 8** and **Chapter 10**.

6.2.3 Failing Scenarios

If an exception occurs while a step is running, the step and ultimately the
scenario will fail so that meaningful test results can be provided.

</> Example #8: Causing a Step to Fail

Before using an assertion library, let's look at how to cause a Cucumber
step to fail.

Ruby

```ruby
Given('this step always fails') do
    raise 'error'
end
```

Java

```java
import io.cucumber.java.en.Given;

public class MySteps {
    @Given("this step always fails")
    public void given_this_step_always_fails() {
        throw new Exception();
    }
}
```

JavaScript

```javascript
const { Given } = require('@cucumber/cucumber');

Given('this step always fails', function () {
    throw new Error();
});
```

6.2.4 Using an Assertion Library

The final step of any automated software test is to validate whether the
application being tested is in the expected state. In order to perform this
validation, we will need to run one or more assertions.

In the previous example, you saw how throwing or raising an exception
within a step definition will cause the scenario to fail. While you can write
your own code to conditionally throw exceptions, there are assertion libraries
that simplify this process and help to keep your code more readable.

</> **Example #9:** Step Definitions with Assertions

◇ **Ruby**

A popular assertion library and test framework for Ruby is RSpec.[32] Run `gem install rspec` to get started.

```ruby
require 'rspec'

When('The users adds {int} to {int}') do |num1, num2|
    @result = num1 + num2
end

Then('the answer should be {int}') do |expected|
    expect(@result).to eq(expected)
end
```

▣ **Java**

You can use the JUnit assertion library with CucumberJVM.

```java
import io.cucumber.java.en.When;
import io.cucumber.java.en.Then;
import org.junit.jupiter.api.Assertions; // for JUnit 4: import org.junit.Assert;

public class AdditionSteps {

    private int result;

    @When("The user adds {int} to {int}")
    public void theUserAdds(int num1, int num2) {
        result = num1 + num2;
    }

    @Then("the answer should be {int}")
    public void theAnswerShouldBe(int expected) {
        Assertions.assertEquals(expected, result); //for JUnit 4: Assert
    }
}
```

▤ **JavaScript**

NodeJS has a built-in assertion library. There are also popular assertion libraries available on NPM such as chai[33] or expect.[34]

```javascript
const { When, Then } = require('@cucumber/cucumber');
const assert = require('assert');

When('The user adds {int} to {int}', function (num1, num2) {
    this.result = num1 + num2;
});

Then('the answer should be {int}', function (expected) {
    assert.strictEqual(this.result, expected);
});
```

---

[32] https://rspec.info/
[33] https://www.npmjs.com/package/chai
[34] https://www.npmjs.com/package/expect

6.3 Step Definition Parameters

In a previous example we looked at a user logging into an application, which
in a realistic test suite would need to support multiple user accounts. In order
to support these situations, you can add parameters to your step definitions.
Instead of writing a step definition for each user, let's add a parameter to
our existing step to support that capability using Cucumber Expressions.[35]
The following types are supported through Cucumber Expressions: `int`,
`float`, `word`, `string`, `anonymous`, `bigdecimal`, `double`, `biginteger`, `byte`,
`short`, `long`.

</> **Example #10:** Cucumber Expressions

◇ **Ruby**

```ruby
require './src/session'

Given('the user {string} logs in') do |user|
    performLogin(user)
end
```

▣ **Java**

```java
import io.cucumber.java.en.Given;
import com.product.app.Session;

public class MySteps {
    @Given("the user {string} logs in")
    public void the_user_string_logs_in(String user) {
        Session.performLogin(user);
    }
}
```

🗊 **JavaScript**

```javascript
const { Given } = require('@cucumber/cucumber');
const { performLogin } = require('../../src/session');

Given('the user {string} logs in', async function(user) {
    await performLogin(user);
});
```

🏅 **Pro Tip:** You can add optional text to your step definitions using
parentheses. For example: `Given there are {int} car(s)`.

⚠ **Caution:** You should use Cucumber Expressions wherever possible
in your step definitions as opposed to Regular Expression matching because Regular Expressions are more difficult to maintain and can introduce
ambiguous step definition errors.

---

[35] https://github.com/cucumber/cucumber-expressions#readme

When you write your tests, you can simply enclose your parameter value
in double quotes and Cucumber will match the step definition text. While
strings are enclosed in double quotes, the number types are not.

```
Feature: The user logs in

Scenario: Fred logs in successfully
    Given the user "Fred" logs in

Scenario: Janet logs in successfully
    Given the user "Janet" logs in
```

</> Example #11: Custom Parameter Types

Besides the built-in types, Cucumber Expressions also support custom types.

◇ Ruby

```ruby
ParameterType(
    name: 'isoDate',
    regexp: /\d{4}-\d{2}-\d{2}/,
    type: Date,
    transformer: ->(date) { Date.parse(date) }
)

When('the user selects the date {isoDate}') do |date|
    # do something with the date...
end
```

▤ Java

```java
import io.cucumber.cucumberexpressions.ParameterType;
import io.cucumber.java.en.When;

public class MySteps {
    @ParameterType("\\d{4}-\\d{2}-\\d{2}")
    public LocalDate isoDate(String date) {
        return LocalDate.parse(date);
    }
    @When("the user selects the date {isoDate}")
    public void the_user_selects_the_date_isodate(LocalDate date) {
        // do something with the date...
    }
}
```

▤ JavaScript

```javascript
const { defineParameterType, When } = require('@cucumber/cucumber');

defineParameterType({
    name: 'isoDate',
    regexp: /\d{4}-\d{2}-\d{2}/,
    transformer: d => new Date(d)
});

When('the user selects the date {isoDate}', async function(date) {
    // do something with the date...
});
```

6.4 Sharing Data between Steps

When a scenario is running, Cucumber will create a scenario context, that exists for the duration of that scenario, and all step definitions have access to this object. This functionality allows for state information regarding the scenario to be shared between steps so that the steps can work together to execute the test. Keep in mind that sharing state across steps can introduce implicit dependencies between step definitions, which could result in unexpected behaviors.

⚠️ **Pitfall:** While sharing data between steps within the context of a scenario allows for more flexible step definitions, each scenario must run independently and not be affected by other scenarios.

🏅 **Pro Tip:** Use the `--order random` flag for Cucumber and CucumberJS or CucumberJVM parameter `cucumber.execution.order=random` to run scenarios in a random order. This will make unintentional coupling between scenarios more obvious.

6.4.1 Sharing Individual Values

If you need to share a few individual values between steps, you can add data directly to the scenario context as needed. For CucumberJVM, you can add private fields to your step class.

</> **Example #12:** Sharing Values between Steps

◇ **Ruby**

```ruby
require './src/session'

Given('the user {string} logs in') do |user|
    performLogin(user)
    @current_user = user
end
```

▣ **Java**

```java
import io.cucumber.java.en.Given;
import com.product.app.Session;

public class MySteps {
    private string currentUser;

    @Given("the user {string} logs in")
    public void the_user_string_logs_in(String user) {
        Session.performLogin(user);
        this.currentUser = user;
    }
}
```

```javascript
const { Given } = require('@cucumber/cucumber');
const { performLogin } = require('../../src/session');

Given('the user {string} logs in', async function(user) {
    await performLogin(user);
    this.currentUser = user;
});
```

6.4.2 The World Object

For more sophisticated test suites, you can define a custom `World` object for your scenarios to use so that you can add data as well as helper functions to your tests. This approach will be used extensively in later examples.

</> Example #13: Using a Custom World Object

◈ Ruby

Create a `CustomWorld` module in Ruby that can contain helper functions you can then access through your step definitions.

In `./features/support/env.rb`:

```ruby
module CustomWorld
    def add_items
        @count ||= 0
        @count += 1
    end
end

World(CustomWorld)
```

In your step definition file:

```ruby
Given('the user adds {int} items to the cart') do |count|
    add_items(count)
end
```

🏅 **Pro Tip:** You can pass multiple module parameters into `World()` and all the helper methods exposed through those modules will be merged together and made available to your step definitions. Additionally, you can add named parameters such as `data: DataModule` if you want the module to be accessible via a specific name in your step definitions:

```ruby
# in your module code:
World(data: DataModule)

# in your step definition code:
Given('the user gets data') do
    the_data = data.get_data
end
```

🅔 Java

While Ruby and JavaScript have built-in support for the `World` object, CucumberJVM requires some additional configuration. You can use dependency injection to automatically load a shared `World` object across any of your step classes. For more information on the dependency injection pattern, refer to **12.1**.

To use dependency injection in your tests, configure a dependency injection library. You can use any dependency injection library of your choice or install PicoContainer in your `./pom.xml` file:

```xml
<dependency>
    <groupId>io.cucumber</groupId>
    <artifactId>cucumber-picocontainer</artifactId>
    <version>7.15.0</version>
    <scope>test</scope>
</dependency>
```

Then create a custom `CustomWorld` class in your test project:

```java
public class CustomWorld {
    private int count = 0;
    public void addItems(int count) {
        this.count += count;
    }
}
```

In your step definition file:

```java
import io.cucumber.java.en.Given;
import com.product.app.test.CustomWorld;

public class MySteps {
    private CustomWorld world;

    public MySteps(CustomWorld world) {
        this.world = world;
    }

    @Given("the user adds {int} items to the cart")
    public void the_user_adds_int_items_to_the_cart(int count) {
        this.world.addItem(count);
    }
}
```

Any step or hook classes in your `./src/test/java/<Pkg Path>` that accept a `CustomWorld` constructor argument will automatically receive an instance of `CustomWorld`, which is created for each scenario in your test run. Once configured, PicoContainer takes care of the rest.

📜 **JavaScript**

You create a `CustomWorld` class in JavaScript that can contain helper functions you can then access through your step definitions. Create a file `./features/support/world.js`:

```javascript
const { setWorldConstructor, World } = require('@cucumber/cucumber');

class CustomWorld extends World {
    constructor(options) {
        super(options);
        this.count = 0;
    }

    addItems(count) {
        this.count += count;
    }
}

setWorldConstructor(CustomWorld);
module.exports = { CustomWorld };
```

Then, in your step definitions:

```javascript
const { When } = require('@cucumber/cucumber');

When('the user adds {int} items to the cart', function(count) {
    this.addItems(count);
});
```

🏅 **Pro Tip:** Consider using TypeScript with CucumberJS to avoid unexpected type issues such as those caused by using dynamically added functions through the scenario context. For an example of using TypeScript with CucumberJS, refer to **10.7**.

🏅 **Pro Tip:** Consider using the `World` class or module instead of dynamically adding properties and functions to your scenario context, especially if you are using TypeScript. As a test suite becomes larger, it can become increasingly difficult to manage helper functions if they aren't organized in a clear and standardized way.

6.5 Organizing Steps into Step Libraries

For larger test suites or scenarios that can be shared across multiple applications, consider creating a step library to maximize code reuse and speed up development of test suites for new applications in an enterprise environment.

🎗 **Pro Tip:** You can host your own internal package repository for storing your packages for RubyGems, Maven, and NPM. For more information on this topic, refer to **Chapter 9**.

6.5.1 Step Libraries for Cucumber (Ruby)

There are two solutions for implementing step libraries in Ruby.

If you don't have the infrastructure to support managing gems, you can use the `--require` command-line flag to load your step library files directly. For example: `cucumber --require ./my_other_steps`. You could combine this solution with a Git submodule to keep the step definitions in their own repository so they can be shared between projects.

⚠ **Pitfall:** Once you use the `--require` flag when calling Cucumber, the `./features` directory will NOT be loaded automatically, and you will have to add a `--require` so that Cucumber still loads your local step definitions.

Alternatively, you can create a Ruby gem for your steps:

1) From a directory where you keep your projects, run `bundle gem <step library name>` and follow the prompts. It will automatically generate a skeleton project for you.
2) Add "gem cucumber" to the `./Gemfile` file in your gem project.
3) Create a file `./lib/<step library name>/step_definitions.rb`; this is where you will put your step definitions.
4) In your test project, add the gem to your project and then add `require('<step library name>/step_definitions')` to your `./features/support/env.rb` file.

⚠ **Pitfall:** Be careful not to sign in to the public RubyGems repository and publish your step library to it if you are not intending to publish your code to the internet. If you're in an enterprise environment where source code needs to be kept internal to your organization, consider setting the `metadata['allowed_push_host']` value in the gem's specification. This is available as of RubyGems version 2.2.0 and above.

6.5.2 Step Libraries for CucumberJVM (Java)

You can create a step library in Java by creating a new package and compiling it as a JAR file.

1) Create a new directory for your step library project.
2) Make another directory `./src/main/java/<Pkg Path>` and put your step definitions here.
3) Create a `./pom.xml` file:

```xml
<?xml version="1.0" encoding="UTF-8"?>
<project xmlns="http://maven.apache.org/POM/4.0.0"
         xmlns:xsi="http://www.w3.org/2001/XMLSchema-instance"
         xsi:schemaLocation="http://maven.apache.org/POM/4.0.0
http://maven.apache.org/xsd/maven-4.0.0.xsd">
    <modelVersion>4.0.0</modelVersion>
    <groupId>com.example.mysteplibrary</groupId>
    <artifactId>my-step-library</artifactId>
    <version>0.0.1</version>
    <properties>
        <java.version>1.8</java.version>
        <project.build.sourceEncoding>UTF-8</project.build.sourceEncoding>
    </properties>
    <dependencies>
        <dependency>
            <groupId>io.cucumber</groupId>
            <artifactId>cucumber-java</artifactId>
            <version>7.15.0</version>
        </dependency>
    </dependencies>
</project>
```

4) Create the JAR file by running `mvn package`.

5) Add the JAR file from your step library to your package repository. If you don't have one, you can get started with a local directory on your machine by adding this section to your `./pom.xml`:

```xml
<repositories>
    <repository>
        <id>local-maven-repo</id>
        <url>file:///C:/local-maven-repo</url>
    </repository>
</repositories>
```

To install the JAR file, run the following command:

```
mvn install:install-file \
   -Dfile=my-step-library.jar \
   -DgroupId=com.example.mysteplibrary \
   -DartifactId=my-step-library \
   -Dversion=0.0.1 \
   -Dpackaging=jar \
   -DlocalRepositoryPath=file:///C:/local-maven-repo
```

6) Add your step library as a dependency for your test project through Maven by updating your `./pom.xml` file in your test project:

```xml
<dependency>
    <groupId>com.example.mysteplibrary</groupId>
    <artifactId>my-step-library</artifactId>
    <version>0.0.1</version>
    <scope>test</scope>
</dependency>
```

7) Run the following command:

`mvn install dependency:copy-dependencies -DskipTests`

This will set up Maven to automatically copy dependencies to your target directory so they are available for use when CucumberJVM runs.

8) Update the "glue" parameter, which specifies one or more classes to scan for step definitions. This parameter is typically specified within an annotation in your `./src/test/java/<Pkg Path>/RunCucumberTest.java` file. It can also be specified with the `-Dcucumber.glue` command-line parameter flag.

Java

```java
package com.example.project1;

import org.junit.platform.suite.api.ConfigurationParameter;
import org.junit.platform.suite.api.IncludeEngines;
import org.junit.platform.suite.api.SelectClasspathResource;
import org.junit.platform.suite.api.Suite;

import static io.cucumber.junit.platform.engine.Constants.PLUGIN_PROPERTY_NAME;
import static io.cucumber.junit.platform.engine.Constants.GLUE_PROPERTY_NAME;

@Suite
@IncludeEngines("cucumber")
@SelectClasspathResource("/features")
@ConfigurationParameter(key = PLUGIN_PROPERTY_NAME, value = "pretty")
@ConfigurationParameter(key = GLUE_PROPERTY_NAME, value = "<Pkg Name>,<Step Lib>")
public class RunCucumberTest {
}
```

⚠ **Pitfall:** Be careful not to sign in to the public Maven central repository and publish your step library to it if you are not intending to publish your code to the internet.

6.5.3 Step Libraries for CucumberJS (JavaScript)

There are two solutions for implementing step libraries in JavaScript.

If you don't have the infrastructure to support managing NPM packages, you can use the `--require` command-line flag to load your step library file directly. For example: `cucumber-js --require ./my_other_steps`. You could combine this solution with a Git submodule to keep the step definitions in their own repository so they can be shared between projects.

Alternatively, you can create an NPM package for your steps:

1) Create a file `./steps.js`; this will be where your entry point and where your steps go.
2) Create a new directory for your project and run `npm init`, then follow the prompts.
3) Run `npm install @cucumber/cucumber` to install CucumberJS.

You can load your step library module in one of two ways:

Option 1: Direct Module Loading In your test project, add the NPM package to your project and then add `require('<NPM package name>')` to a JS file in `./features/support/`. When you use `require()`, if the file hasn't been loaded by `NodeJS` yet, it will execute that file.

Option 2: Using the Command-Line You can use the `--require-module` command-line flag to automatically load your module.

🏅 **Pro Tip:** If you want to have more than one step definitions file in your step library project, you can separate them and then include `require()` calls for each of your other files in `./steps.js` so that when the entry point file is loaded, it will then load your other step files.

⚠️ **Pitfall:** Be careful not to sign in to the public NPM repository and publish your step library to it if you are not intending to publish your step definitions to the internet. If you're in an enterprise environment where source code needs to be kept internal to your organization, consider setting the `publishConfig` value in the `./package.json` of your package. You can also set `"private": true` to prevent NPM from allowing the package to be published at all.

6.6 Using Hooks

Earlier we looked at using the `Background` keyword in Gherkin to run setup code for every scenario in a feature file. While this is useful for cases where setting up your application is explicitly part of the scenario, there are many other cases where you want setup and teardown code to run for each scenario without being visible in your feature files, such as when opening and closing database connections, starting and stopping WebDriver, or creating or cleaning up files. The different versions of Cucumber offer hooks to support this capability.

 **Example #14:** Using Cucumber Hooks

6.6.1 Before and After a Scenario

All versions of Cucumber support `Before` and `After` hooks.

 **Ruby**

Besides `Before` and `After`, Cucumber in Ruby lets you wrap a scenario run using the `Around` hook for tasks like custom error handling or timeouts.

```ruby
Before do |scenario|
    # run code before each scenario.
end

After do |scenario|
    # run code after each scenario.
end

Around do |scenario, block|
    # run code before each scenario.
    block.call
    # run code after each scenario.
end
```

⚠️ **Caution:** The `Around` hook wraps a whole scenario, not each step.

Java

```java
import io.cucumber.java.After;
import io.cucumber.java.Before;
import io.cucumber.java.Scenario;

public class Hooks {
    @Before
    public void setupTest(Scenario scenario) {
        // run code before each scenario.
    }

    @After
    public void teardownTest(Scenario scenario) {
        // run code after each scenario.
    }
}
```

📜 JavaScript

```javascript
const { After, Before } = require('@cucumber/cucumber');

Before(function (scenario) {
    // run code before each scenario.
});

After(function (scenario) {
    // run code after each scenario.
});
```

6.6.2 Before and After Running Tests

💎 Ruby

In Ruby there is no hook for running code at the start of a test run because you simply write your code somewhere in the `./features/support` directory and it will run before your tests. You can use the `at_exit` hook to run code when the test run is finished.

```ruby
# run code before all scenarios.
at_exit do
    # run code after all scenarios.
end
```

☕ Java

```java
import io.cucumber.java.AfterAll;
import io.cucumber.java.BeforeAll;

public class Hooks {
    @BeforeAll
    public static void setup() {
        // run code before all scenarios.
    }

    @AfterAll
    public static void teardown() {
        // run code after all scenarios.
    }
}
```

📜 JavaScript

```javascript
const { AfterAll, BeforeAll } = require('@cucumber/cucumber');

BeforeAll(function () {
    // run code before all scenarios.
});

AfterAll(function () {
    // run code after all scenarios.
});
```

6.6.3 Before and After a Step

◇ Ruby

There is no `BeforeStep` hook in Ruby, but there is an `AfterStep` hook.

```ruby
AfterStep do |scenario|
    # run code after each step of a scenario.
end
```

🏅 **Pro Tip:** If you want to have a `BeforeStep` hook for Ruby, you can create a **transformer** function and wrap your step definitions with it. You can then create a custom hook function to register and execute callbacks. For examples of this, refer to **Chapter 10**.

▣ Java

```java
import io.cucumber.java.AfterStep;
import io.cucumber.java.BeforeStep;
import io.cucumber.java.Scenario;

public class Hooks {
    @BeforeStep
    public void setupTestStep(Scenario scenario) {
        // run code before each step of a scenario.
    }

    @AfterStep
    public void teardownTestStep(Scenario scenario) {
        // run code after each step of a scenario.
    }
}
```

▤ JavaScript

```javascript
const { AfterStep, BeforeStep } = require('@cucumber/cucumber');

BeforeStep(function () {
    // run code before each scenario.
});

AfterStep(function () {
    // run code after each scenario.
});
```

6.6.4 Conditional Hooks

Not all scenarios or features require the same setup and teardown tasks, so you can combine hooks with tag expressions to implement conditional hooks based on the scenario tags associated with the scenarios in your test suite.

💠 Ruby

```ruby
Before('@smoke and @ui') do |scenario|
    # run code before each scenario.
end

After('@smoke and @ui') do |scenario|
    # run code after each scenario.
end
```

🗐 Java

```java
import io.cucumber.java.After;
import io.cucumber.java.Before;
import io.cucumber.java.Scenario;

public class Hooks {
    @Before("@smoke and @ui")
    public void setupTest(Scenario scenario) {
        // run code before each scenario.
    }

    @After("@smoke and @ui")
    public void teardownTest(Scenario scenario) {
        // run code after each scenario.
    }
}
```

🗎 JavaScript

```javascript
const { After, Before } = require('@cucumber/cucumber');

Before({ tags: '@smoke and @ui' }, function (scenario) {
    // run code before each scenario.
});

After({ tags: '@smoke and @ui' }, function (scenario) {
    // run code after each scenario.
});
```

🏅 **Pro Tip:** The `scenario` parameter contains scenario-specific context information such as the name of the scenario, the status of the test case, and the scenario tags associated with the scenario. Refer to specific documentation for Ruby,[36] Java,[37] and JavaScript.[38]

---

[36] https://www.rubydoc.info/gems/cucumber/8.0.0
[37] https://javadoc.io/doc/io.cucumber/cucumber-java
[38] https://github.com/cucumber/cucumber-js/blob/main/docs

6.7 Using Data Tables

Adding parameters to your step definitions is an effective way of building reusable steps so you can write Gherkin scenarios for your application without having to write new step definitions as frequently once your step library is established. While `string` and `number` parameters are useful, sometimes scenarios require more complex inputs. For these cases, Gherkin supports passing data table parameters outside the step name itself.

</> Example #15: Data Table Parameters

```
Feature: Demonstrate Data Tables

Scenario: Using a Data Table Parameter
    Given the following users are created:
    | id | name   |
    | 1  | Jim    |
    | 2  | Amanda |
```

Notice how the data table parameter looks similar to a scenario outline example as they are both two-dimensional tables represented in Gherkin, even though they are used for different purposes. Instead of executing multiple examples of a scenario, the data table parameter is passed to your step definition as a function argument with all the rows and columns available to your code.

◇ Ruby

The data table parameter is passed as an argument to your Ruby step definition function. The `table` argument contains a `hashes` array where each element is an object with a key/value pair for each column in the row.[39]

```
Given('the following users are created:') do |table|
    table.hashes.each_value { |v| puts v }
end
```

⊟ Java

The data table parameter is passed as an argument to your Java step definition method. The `DataTable` class allows you to convert the table into a `List` containing `Map` values.[40]

---

[39] https://www.rubydoc.info/github/cucumber/cucumber-ruby/Cucumber/MultilineArgument/DataTable

[40] https://javadoc.io/doc/io.cucumber/datatable

Create a file `./src/test/java/<Pkg Path>/MySteps.java`:

```java
import io.cucumber.java.en.Given;
import io.cucumber.java.DataTable;
import java.util.List;
import java.util.Map;

public class MySteps {
    @Given("the following users are created:")
    public void the_following_users_are_created(DataTable table) {
        List<Map<String, String>> rows = table.asMaps(String.class, String.class);
        for (Map<String, String> row : rows) {
            row.forEach((key, value) -> System.out.println(key + ": " + value));
        }
    }
}
```

Additionally, you can define custom data table types in CucumberJVM the same way you can define custom parameter types.[41]

```java
import com.product.app.User;
import io.cucumber.java.en.Given;
import io.cucumber.java.DataTable;
import java.util.List;
import java.util.Map;

public class MySteps {

    @DataTableType
    public User users(Map<String, String> entry) {
        return new User(
            entry.get("id"),
            entry.get("name"));
    }

    @Given("the following users are created:")
    public void the_following_users_are_created(List<User> users) {
        for (User user : users) {
            System.out.println(user.toString());
        }
    }
}
```

JavaScript

The data table parameter is passed as an argument to your JavaScript step definition function. The `table` argument contains a `hashes` function that returns an array where each element is an object with a key/value pair for each column in the row.[42]

```javascript
const { Given } = require('@cucumber/cucumber');

Given('the following users are created:', async function(table) {
    table.hashes().forEach((row) => console.log(JSON.stringify(row)));
});
```

---

[41] https://cucumber.io/docs/cucumber/configuration/?lang=java
[42] https://github.com/cucumber/cucumber-js/blob/main/docs/support_files

6.8 Using Docstrings

Another type of special parameter supported by Gherkin is docstring, which allows you to pass a multiline string to a step. Additionally, you can specify the content type.

</> Example #16: Docstring Parameters

```gherkin
Feature: Demonstrate Docstrings

Scenario: Using a Docstring Parameter
    Given some multiline text is typed into the screen:
        """
        line 1...
        line 2...
        line 3...
        more....
        """
```

Pro Tip: You can also use the backtick character (`` ` ``) instead of double quotes for specifying docstrings in Gherkin.

Ruby

The docstring parameter is passed as an argument to your Ruby step definition function.

```ruby
Given('some multiline text is typed into the screen:') do |text|
    puts text
end
```

Java

The docstring parameter is passed as an argument to your Java step definition method.

```java
import io.cucumber.java.en.Given;

public class MySteps {
    @Given("some multiline text is typed into the screen:")
    public void some_multi_line_text_is_typed(String text) {
        System.out.println(text);
    }
}
```

Additionally, you can define custom docstring types in CucumberJVM the
same way you can define custom parameter types.[43]

```java
import com.fasterxml.jackson.core.JsonProcessingException;
import com.fasterxml.jackson.databind.JsonNode;
import com.fasterxml.jackson.databind.ObjectMapper;
import io.cucumber.java.DocStringType;
import io.cucumber.java.en.Given;

public class MySteps {
    private static ObjectMapper objectMapper = new ObjectMapper();

    @DocStringType
    public JsonNode json(String text) throws JsonProcessingException {
        return objectMapper.readValue(text, JsonNode.class);
    }

    @Given("the following JSON data is entered:")
    public void the_following_json_data_is_entered(JsonNode books) {
        // step code goes here...
    }
}
```

You can use a custom type by specifying the content type in Gherkin:

```gherkin
Feature: Demonstrate Custom Docstring Types

Scenario: Using Docstring custom types
    Given the following JSON data is entered:
      """json
      {
        "key1": "value1",
        "key2": "value2",
        "key3": "value3"
      }
      """
```

JavaScript

The docstring parameter is passed as an argument to your JavaScript step
definition function.

```javascript
const { Given } = require('@cucumber/cucumber');

Given('some multiline text is typed into the screen:', async function(text) {
    console.log(text);
});
```

---

[43] https://cucumber.io/docs/cucumber/configuration/?lang=java

Chapter 7: Writing Scenarios

Once you have an initial set of step definitions, you can start writing scenarios that can be executed as part of automated testing and CI/CD.

7.1 Setting Up Feature Files

Before writing scenarios, you will need to have one or more feature files to write scenarios in. In this section, we'll review how to organize your feature files and also what information should be included.

7.1.1 Organizing Your Features

There are different ways to organize your feature files. Let's take a look at some options:

 **Anti-pattern:** Organizing by Story or Task

If you're using an issue tracking tool, it can be tempting to create feature files that match each of the stories or tasks you have assigned to your application. While some issue tracking tools such as Rally have a concept of "features" that you could create feature files based on, oftentimes the scope of a feature file is not the same as a user story or task, so organizing feature files in this way can cause confusion in the long term. Remember, feature files should always refer to a *feature* (hence the name) of your application.

🏅 **Pro Tip:** Instead of basing feature files off user stories or tasks, use scenario tags to map your scenarios and features to user stories and tasks. Additionally, consider pushing test reports from Cucumber to your issue tracking tool. For more information, refer to **9.4 Integrating Test Reporting**.

By Feature While organizing feature files by feature seems like the most obvious approach, agile methodology does not define clear distinctions between user stories, epics, and features, so it can be somewhat confusing to implement. For the purpose of this discussion, a feature will be considered a quantifiable piece of functionality within your application that is supported by one or more business rules.

By Component You can also organize your feature files by component based on the structure of your application. If you're writing UI tests, you could have a directory within `./features` for each area of your application's UI with features underneath each directory. Alternatively, if you are testing HTTP endpoints, each feature file could represent a related set of endpoints. Organizing your feature files by component depends on the type of testing that you are performing (e.g., the Testing Pyramid) and what type of application you are testing.

🏅 **Pro Tip:** Consider combining both of these approaches, where you create directories for each component of your application in the `./features` directory and then each of those component directories can have feature files associated with a feature of your application.

7.1.2 Writing a Feature File

Once you create an empty text file with a `.feature` extension, the first step in writing a feature file is adding the `Feature` line at the top. Here, you can provide a one-sentence description with the feature on the first line and then add additional information below the `Feature` line. If you are using agile methodology for managing the software development process, your description below the `Feature` line should be written in the following form:[44]

```
As a <role> \ I want <something> \ so that <reason>
```

For more information on agile methodology, refer to the **Further Reading** section.

You can also add scenario tags above the `Feature` line that will be associated with all rules and scenarios in the feature file. Consider reviewing the scenario tags that you designed and standardized in **4.5 Defining Special Scenario Tags**. In this example, let's mark all scenarios in a feature file with the `@functional` and `@ui` tags to indicate that these are functional UI tests:

```
@functional @ui
Feature: The User Can Login to the Application
    As a user
    I want to login to the application
    So that I can have access to the application

# Scenarios go after this...
```

7.1.3 Your First Scenario

Now that we have an established a feature file with the appropriate scenario tags and documentation added, let's write a scenario.

```
@APP-STORY-001
Scenario: The user logs in successfully
    Given the user navigates to the home page
    When the user "test user 1" logs in
    Then the user should be logged in
```

---

[44]https://www.mountaingoatsoftware.com/agile/user-stories

7.2 Using Scenario Outlines

Writing your examples as scenario outlines can allow you to focus on writing new variations of existing scenarios instead of starting over every time.

7.2.1 Basic Scenario Outlines

Consider the following example where we have multiple invalid users that we want to test:

</> **Example #17:** Writing a Scenario Outline

```
Scenario Outline: The user does not log in successfully
    Given the user navigates to the home page
    When the user "<invalid user>" logs in
    Then the user is not signed in
Examples:
| invalid user |
|  bad user 1  |
|  bad user 2  |
|  bad user 3  |
```

When this feature file is executed in Cucumber, three scenarios will be run: one for each row in the `Examples` table. Notice how the placeholder `<invalid user>` matches the table column "invalid user": Cucumber will iterate through the rows of the table looking for matching column names and then substitute them with the appropriate value for each scenario run. You can put the placeholders anywhere within the scenario's steps.

🛑 **Anti-pattern:** Using scenario outline placeholders to replace step definition text outside of parameters.

```
Scenario Outline: Anti-pattern version of login test.
    Given the user navigates to the home page
    When the user "<user>" logs in
    Then the user <status> signed in
Examples:
| user       | status |
|     user 1 |   is   |
| bad user 1 | is not |
```

Several issues can arise from using placeholders in this way. First, this can cause warnings in your text editor if you're using an IDE that supports auto-complete. It's also confusing and therefore likely to be misunderstood by nontechnical members of your team, negating one of the primary advantages to using a language such as Gherkin in the first place. Placeholders should only be used for step definition parameters or within a table parameter (only the values though, not the column names).

⚠️ **Pitfall:** If a scenario outline doesn't have at least one `Examples` table with at least one row in it, no tests will be executed, which may not be expected or obvious at first when looking at your feature file.

7.2.2 Scenario Outlines with Multiple Examples Sections

One of the more advanced features of scenario outlines is the ability to have multiple "Examples" sections. Let's say you would like to tag all of your scenarios with story numbers from your work item tracking tool like Jira or Rally, and you also want to use scenario outlines to avoid copy/pasting steps. How do you tag each set of examples within the scenario outline with the different scenario tags?

</> Example #18: Using Multiple Examples Sections

You can use multiple examples as shown below:

```
Scenario Outline: The user does not log in successfully
    Given the user navigates to the home page
    When the user "<invalid user>" logs in
    Then the user is not signed in

@APP-STORY-001
Examples:
| invalid user |
|  bad user 1  |

@APP-STORY-002
Examples:
| invalid user |
|  bad user 2  |

@APP-STORY-003
Examples:
| invalid user |
|  bad user 3  |
```

Even if you anticipate that a scenario will only ever have one example, sometimes it is still advantageous to use a scenario outline to keep test parameters organized and more clearly identified at the bottom of your scenario.

Pro Tip: As your application grows, there will be defects that are logged by users and internal testing. Always add a scenario or an example to an existing scenario outline to validate that the defect is fixed and remains fixed into the future. Testing defects is an important part of regression testing. Also, if you have defect numbers from your issue tracking tool, add them as scenario tags so you can track the status of defects.

7.3 Using Backgrounds

While `Scenario Outline` can be useful for organizing a set of tests with the same steps but different parameters, there are also cases where all the scenarios in your feature file start with the same steps, but the `When` and `Then` steps are different. Instead of copy/pasting the same `Given` steps repeatedly, you can use `Background`:

</> Example #19: The `Background` keyword

Without `Background`:

```
Feature: Customers can perform actions in the online store.

Scenario: Customers can add an item to the cart
Given the user "Jim" logs in
And the user navigates to the "home" page
When the user adds an item to their shopping cart
Then an item should appear in the user's shopping cart

Scenario: Customers can search for an item
Given the user "Jim" logs in
And the user navigates to the "home" page
When the user searches for item "item 1"
Then item "item 1" should appear in search results
```

Using `Background`:

```
Feature: Customers can perform actions in the online store.

Background:
Given the user "Jim" logs in
And the user navigates to the "home" page

Scenario: Customers can add an item to the cart
When the user adds an item to their shopping cart
Then an item should appear in the user's shopping cart

Scenario: Customers can search for an item
When the user searches for item "item 1"
Then item "item 1" should appear in search results
```

Any steps added to `Background` will be run first for all scenarios within the given feature file.

🏅 **Pro Tip:** Make sure that the wording of the steps in `Background` describes the functional requirements of the feature. Otherwise, consider using conditional hooks for loading scenario data in a less visible way. Take the time to decide whether certain scenario startup tasks are part of your application's business rules or purely technical in nature.

7.4 Using Rules

A relatively new feature of Gherkin is the `Rule` keyword that allows you
to create multiple groups of scenarios within a feature file. While you
do not have to use rules in your feature files, they are a helpful way of
keeping your scenarios more organized without having to break out your
tests into multiple files. Besides being used for organizing scenarios, you
can add scenario tags and a `Background` section to each of your rules. This
functionality is available as of Gherkin 6, so you will want to confirm that
your version of Cucumber supports this functionality before adding rules to
your feature files.

‹/› Example #20: Using `Background` with `Rule`

You can have multiple `Background` sections within a feature file by placing
a `Background` within a `Rule`. Any scenarios within the `Rule` will have the
`Background` section of that `Rule` executed before each scenario.

```
Feature: Customers can perform actions in the online store.

  Rule: Jim Logs In

    Background:
      Given the user "Jim" logs in
      And the user navigates to the "home" page

    Scenario: Customers can add an item to the cart
      When the user adds an item to their shopping cart
      Then an item should appear in the user's shopping cart

    Scenario: Customers can search for an item
      When the user searches for item "item 1"
      Then item "item 1" should appear in search results
```

From the perspective of your application's requirements, rules in Gherkin
represent business rules where the feature of an application would contain
one or more rules, each with their own scenarios. This extra layer of
organization can be used to keep test suites tidier and avoid excessively
large scenarios.

7.5 Using Scenario Tags

Most test frameworks have a concept of "labels" or "tags" within their design. In Gherkin, scenario tags are a powerful feature of Gherkin that allows you to categorize and filter scenarios. This flexibility enhances the manageability of your test suite and provides a straightforward approach to managing test execution. There are a few different places where scenario tags can be used in a feature file:

- **Feature**: Tags all scenarios within a feature file
- **Rule**: Tags all scenarios within a *rule*
- **Scenario**: Tags a specific scenario
- **Scenario Outline**: Tags all examples within a scenario outline
- **Scenario Outline Example**: Tags one or more examples within a scenario outline

</> Example #21: Scenario Tag Types

```
@feature-level-tag
Feature: You can place scenario tags in all scenarios within a feature.

  @rule-level-tag
  Rule: You can place scenario tags on all scenarios within a rule.
    Note that rules are optional.

    @scenario-level-tag
    Scenario: You can also place tags directly on a scenario
      # ...

@scenario-outline-level-tag
Scenario Outline: You can place tags on all examples of a scenario outline
    # ...

@scenario-outline-example-level-tag
Examples:
    | param  |
    | value1 |

@scenario-outline-example-level-tag
Examples:
    | param  |
    | value2 |
```

These scenario tags can become a powerful way of categorizing and managing test suites by combining them with tag expressions and hooks. For more information, refer to **Chapter 4** and **Chapter 6**.

7.6 Language Localization Support

While many examples of Gherkin presented in books or on the internet are written in English, feature files can be written in other languages. Let's take a look at how localization works with Cucumber: Add the `language` comment header at the top of a feature file to specify the spoken language to use. Also, some versions of Cucumber support additional language-specific functionality such as language-specific bindings.

</> Example #22: Writing a Scenario in Spanish

```
# language: es

Necesidad del negocio: Los clientes pueden iniciar sesión en la tienda online.
    Puedo escribir lo que quiera aquí, esto es para humanos.

@una-etiqueta @otra-etiqueta
Escenario: El usuario no inicia sesión correctamente
    Dado que el usuario navega a la página de inicio
    Cuando el usuario "John" inicia sesión
    Entonces el usuario no debería iniciar sesión.
```

Cucumber (Ruby)

You can get a list of all supported languages by running `cucumber --i18n-languages` or get the translation information for a specific language by running `cucumber --i18n-keywords <lang>`.

CucumberJVM (Java)

You can use language-specific annotation classes for your step definitions.

Java

```java
import io.cucumber.java.es.Cuando;

public class MySteps {
    @Cuando("el usuario {string} inicia sesión")
    public void when_the_user_string_logs_in(String user) {
        Session.performLogin(user);
    }
}
```

CucumberJS (JavaScript)

You can get a list of all supported languages by running `cucumber-js --i18n-languages` or get the translation information for a specific language by running `cucumber-js --i18n-keywords <lang>`. You can also set the default language when running tests using `cucumber-js --language <lang>`.

Chapter 8: Improving Performance

Once your test suite begins to grow in size, you may start to experience performance problems. This is normal for any growing piece of software and there are many ways to improve efficiency and reduce test duration for your automation.

8.1 Handling Timeouts and Retries

As the number of components that your tests interact with increases, you can expect test durations to increase while also becoming more unpredictable. Because of this increase in complexity, sometimes a test is going to have to wait for the application you're testing to perform an operation, causing further uncertainty and potential timing problems.

 **Anti-pattern:** "wait sprinkles"

A naive approach to addressing timing difficulties is to use `sleep()` for some predetermined (i.e., arbitrary) number of seconds to pause execution before continuing the test in an attempt to improve test stability. I refer to this approach as "wait sprinkles" because I have observed that many developers writing automation simply "sprinkle" the "waits" into their code wherever tests fail because of timing problems. While adding these pauses in the code can temporarily fix reliability problems within your tests, it ultimately slows down the performance of your automation and causes reliability issues in the long term. When you invest in properly writing and maintaining your tests, you will receive the benefits in perpetuity. Conversely, quick fixes will ultimately result in technical debt, which will then require more time and effort in the future to fix than would have been required to implement a permanent fix in the first place.

8.1.1 Enforcing Timeouts

Before addressing the problem of wait sprinkles, we need to consider how to enforce boundaries when interacting with external systems: your tests cannot assume that the application will respond as expected or ever respond at all. If your application doesn't respond in a timely manner while under test, then the test needs to automatically fail after a specified amount of time by using a timeout. You can enforce timeout rules globally by overriding the default timeout values that Cucumber uses for step definitions if your programming language variant of Cucumber supports timeouts. Otherwise, you can add timeouts to your step definitions directly.

</> Example #23: Enforcing Timeouts in Step Definitions

◆ Ruby

This implementation of Cucumber does not have timeouts built into it; however, you can use the `timeout` gem[45] to set them yourself. To get started, run `gem install timeout` and then modify your `.rb` file:

```ruby
require 'timeout'

# apply the timeout for each scenario:
Around do |scenario, block|
    Timeout.timeout(30) do
        block.call
    end
end

# apply the timeout to a specific step:
Given 'some step that needs a timeout' do
    Timeout.timeout(30) do
        # your step definition code...
    end
end
```

Alternatively, you can set timeouts at the application or block level if you're using a UI testing library such as Capybara:[46]

```ruby
# create a global custom driver with your timeout built into it.
Capybara.register_driver :custom_firefox_driver do |app|
    client = Selenium::WebDriver::Remote::Http::Default.new
    client.timeout = 120
    Capybara::Selenium::Driver.new(app,
                                   browser: :firefox,
                                   http_client: client)
end
Capybara.default_driver = :custom_firefox_driver

# ...or set timeouts at the block level.
Capybara.using_wait_time 30 do # ... searching for page elements, etc.
end
```

For more information about Capybara, refer to **11.4.3**.

---

[45] https://github.com/ruby/timeout
[46] https://github.com/teamcapybara/capybara

📇 Java

CucumberJVM does not have built-in support for timeouts. However, you can use additional Java libraries such as Awaitility.[47] To get started, update your `./pom.xml`:

```xml
<dependency>
    <groupId>org.awaitility</groupId><artifactId>awaitility</artifactId>
    <version>4.2.1</version><scope>test</scope>
</dependency>
```

Then, in your step definition file:

```java
import io.cucumber.java.en.Then;
import java.util.concurrent.*;
import org.awaitility.Awaitility.*;

public class MySteps {
    @Then("some long-running assertion is performed")
    public void then_some_long_running_assertion_is_performed() {
        await().atMost(60, TimeUnit.SECONDS).until(() -> { /* <your code> */ });
    }
}
```

📜 JavaScript

CucumberJS allows you to set timeouts per step definition:

```javascript
const { Given } = require('@cucumber/cucumber');

Given('the user does something', { timeout: 60000 }, async function() {
    // step definition code goes here...
});
```

It is also possible to globally set the timeout for all step definitions. However, I recommend setting the timeout on each step definition since some I/O-based steps may need more time than others (HTTP calls versus reading from the file system for example).

```javascript
const { setDefaultTimeout } = require('@cucumber/cucumber');
setDefaultTimeout(60000);
```

🏅 **Pro Tip:** Consider setting timeout and retry values in your test configuration. For more information, refer to **10.1**.

8.1.2 Implementing Step Retries

Now that you have added timeouts to your steps, you can begin to consider how to improve the performance of assertions that depend on the state of your application. When interacting with an external system, you should have retries on your assertions along with a timeout. While more complex than a `sleep()` call, this implementation improves the reliability of your

---

[47]https://github.com/awaitility/awaitility

tests while remaining performant. When performing retries, use an automatic back-off, which is when the wait time between each retry increases exponentially to reduce excessive polling against the external system. There are libraries available across many programming languages that support retry functionality, including advanced features such as automatic back-off.

</> Example #24: Implementing Retries in Step Definitions

◇ Ruby

There is a Retries gem[48] that can be used to implement retries. To get started, run **gem install retries** and update your step definitions:

```ruby
require 'retries'

with_retries(
    max_tries: 10,
    rescue: [StandardError],
    base_sleep_seconds: 0.1,
    max_sleep_seconds: 2.0
) do
    # code which may require retries
end
```

▣ Java

You can perform retries in Java with Failsafe.[49] To get started, update your `pom.xml`:

```xml
<dependency>
    <groupId>dev.failsafe</groupId><artifactId>failsafe</artifactId>
    <version>3.3.2</version><scope>test</scope>
</dependency>
```

Then, in your step definition file:

```java
import dev.failsafe.*;
import java.time.Duration;
import java.time.temporal.ChronoUnit;

class MyClass {
    public static void runTest() {
        RetryPolicy<Object> retryPolicy = RetryPolicy.builder()
            .withMaxRetries(10)
            .withDelay(Duration.ofSeconds(1))
            .withBackoff(100, 2000, ChronoUnit.MILLIS)
            .build();

        Failsafe.with(retryPolicy).run(() -> {
            // code which may require retries.
        });
    }
}
```

---

[48] https://github.com/ooyala/retries
[49] https://github.com/failsafe-lib/failsafe

🗊 JavaScript

With modern NodeJS, I/O-based functions are typically marked **async** and return a **Promise**.[50] You can implement retries using promise-retry.[51] To get started, run **npm install promise-retry**. In your step definition file:

```javascript
const promiseRetry = require('promise-retry');
const options = {
    retries: 10,
    factor: 2,
    minTimeout: 100,
    maxTimeout: 2000,
};

promiseRetry(async function (retry) {
    try {
        // code which may require retries.
    }
    catch (ex) {
        // add additional logic here in order to conditionally retry.
        retry();
    }
}, options);
```

⚠️ **Pitfall:** Avoid using arrow functions[52] with CucumberJS step definitions since arrow functions bind **this** to the parent scope automatically,[53] which prevents you from accessing the scenario context object.

8.1.3 Implementing Scenario Retries

Besides performing retries at the step or I/O operation level, Cucumber can also retry failing scenarios automatically. While retrying whole scenarios actually increases the current test duration, in a CI/CD pipeline, getting a passing build instead of failing because of a flaky test can ultimately save time. Keep in mind that while allowing flaky scenarios to pass a build can help improve build outcomes and save time, your team still needs to take the time to fix these problematic tests so that they don't need to be rerun.

⚠️ **Pitfall:** Do not use scenario retries in combination with fail fast as you will unpredictably skip scenarios during your test run, resulting in invalid test results. It is important to carefully consider the side effects of any actions being taken above the scenario level of execution and how those decisions affect the validity of your tests, especially with CI/CD.

</> Example #25: Using the Retry Flag

The simplest way to implement retries is by using the **retry** flag.

---

[50] https://developer.mozilla.org/en-US/docs/Web/JavaScript/Guide/Using_promises
[51] https://www.npmjs.com/package/promise-retry
[52] https://javascript.info/arrow-functions
[53] https://github.com/cucumber/cucumber-js/blob/main/docs/faq.md

◇ Ruby

You can use the `--retry <attempts>` flag to retry any failing scenarios a specified number of times. You can also use the `--retry-total <attempts>` flag to specify a limit to how many total scenarios can fail.

▣ Java

While CucumberJVM does not have its own `--retry` flag, there is a configuration option for the Maven Surefire plugin `rerunFailingTestsCount` that allows you to set how many times to retry failing tests. You can set this flag either through the command-line when calling Maven using `-Dsurefire.rerunFailingTestsCount=1` or through your `./pom.xml` file:

```
<configuration>
    <rerunFailingTestsCount>1</rerunFailingTestsCount>
</configuration>
```

▤ JavaScript

You can use the `--retry <attempts>` flag to retry any failing scenarios a specified number of times. There is also a `--retry-tag-filter <exp>` flag that uses tag expressions to limit which scenarios can be retried. You must specify the `--retry` flag in order to use `--retry-tag-filter`.

`</>` Example #26: Using the Rerun Formatter

Another approach for implementing scenario retries in Cucumber is the `rerun` formatter. When you run your tests, you can have all failed scenarios outputted to a text file, which can then be passed into another test run. While more complicated than using the `--retry` flag, this approach gives you more fine-grained control over retries and additional metrics to capture.

For both Ruby and JavaScript, you can use the `-f` or `--format` flag in combination with `--out` to produce a `./rerun.txt` file: `-f rerun --out rerun.txt`. Then you can rerun Cucumber or CucumberJS with `@<rerun file path>`: `cucumber @rerun.txt`. With Java, you can specify the formatter and rerun options via command-line or using your `./pom.xml` file: `mvn test -Dcucumber.plugin="rerun:rerun.txt"` followed by `mvn test -Dcucumber.features="@rerun.txt"`.

If you take the time to utilize these approaches within your tests in the early phases of the development process, your tests will be able to scale better over time as the size and complexity of your test suite inevitably increases. Utilizing retries can also improve the performance of your tests while simultaneously improving their reliability, especially for traditionally flaky types of testing such as UI automation.

8.2 Running Scenarios in Parallel

For test suites that have a lot of I/O operations or are testing a UI, running
scenarios in parallel can be a viable way of improving performance at the
expense of memory and CPU usage. This approach will not be effective at
improving performance for component tests, especially if the components
being tested are performing CPU-intensive operations.

◈ Ruby

Cucumber itself does not support parallel execution in Ruby, but there
are additional tools that can be used to run your scenarios in parallel such
as `parallel_tests`. To get started, run `gem install parallel_tests`[54]
and then use the terminal:

```
parallel_cucumber -n 2 -o '<cucumber command-line flags>'
```

You can differentiate which instance your tests are executing in by using
`ENV['TEST_ENV_NUMBER']`. Keep in mind that `parallel_tests` can only
run in parallel at the feature level, not per scenario.

▣ Java

For JUnit 4:

There is limited support for parallel test execution in JUnit 4. You can only
run in parallel per feature file, not per scenario. If you're using the Failsafe
or Surefire Maven plugins, add the following to your configuration:

```
<configuration>
    <parallel>methods</parallel><threadCount>4</threadCount>
    <perCoreThreadCount>false</perCoreThreadCount>
</configuration>
```

For JUnit 5:

```
// ... other annotations ...
@ConfigurationParameter(key = "cucumber.execution.parallel.enabled", value = true)
@ConfigurationParameter(
    key = "cucumber.execution.parallel.config.strategy", value = "fixed")
@ConfigurationParameter(
    key = "cucumber.execution.parallel.config.fixed.parallelism", value = 4)
public class RunCucumberTest {
}
```

🏅 **Pro Tip:** Use Maven profiles to manage parallel settings instead of
coding them. Refer to **10.1.2** for more information.

There are additional options, including dynamic parallelization
based on the number of available cores on the current machine.[55]
You can even define a custom parallelization strategy using the

---

[54] https://github.com/grosser/parallel_tests
[55] https://javadoc.io/doc/io.cucumber/cucumber-junit-platform-engine

`cucumber.execution.parallel.config.custom.class` option by implementing the `ParallelExecutionConfigurationStrategy` interface.

You can also assign scenario tags to specific resources in order to avoid resource contention across threads.

```java
// ... other annotations ...
@ConfigurationParameter(
    key = "cucumber.execution.exclusive-resources.reads-props.read",
    value = "java.lang.System.properties")
@ConfigurationParameter(
    key = "cucumber.execution.exclusive-resources.reads-and-writes-props.read-write",
    value = "java.lang.System.properties")
public class RunCucumberTest {
}
```

If you want a scenario to run in complete isolation, add the following configuration:

```java
// ... other annotations ...
@ConfigurationParameter(
key = "cucumber.execution.exclusive-resources.isolated.read-write",
value =
"org.junit.platform.engine.support.hierarchical.ExclusiveResource.GLOBAL_KEY")
public class RunCucumberTest {
}
```

Now, in your feature file, you can identify which resources need to be locked for each scenario:

```gherkin
@reads-props
Scenario: A scenario which reads system properties
    # steps...

@reads-and-writes-props
Scenario: A scenario which reads and writes system properties
    # steps...

@isolated
Scenario: A scenario which runs in complete isolation
    # steps...
```

JavaScript

The CucumberJS CLI supports running scenarios in parallel using the `--parallel <count>` flag. Since NodeJS is single threaded, CucumberJS will spawn multiple processes. Each worker process will receive the environment variables `CUCUMBER_PARALLEL=true`, `CUCUMBER_TOTAL_WORKERS=<number>`, and `CUCUMBER_WORKER_ID=<number>`. If you want more control over how scenarios are executed, use the `setParallelCanAssign` function:

```javascript
import { setParallelCanAssign, parallelCanAssignHelpers } from '@cucumber/cucumber';
setParallelCanAssign(parallelCanAssignHelpers.atMostOnePicklePerTag(['@isolated']));
```

8.3 Limiting Which Tests Are Run

An obvious way of improving the performance of your automated testing is
to simply run less testing. While simple in premise, in practice it is difficult
to correctly determine which scenarios you can skip without reducing the
efficacy of your tests and the quality of your application. As we look at some
different ways to tackle this problem, you will see that there are trade-offs
to each solution that you will need to evaluate and consider for your own
projects.

8.3.1 Fail Fast

If you want a simple and reliable way of improving the performance of your
tests without making complex decisions about which tests to run, then fail
fast is a viable solution to consider. When fail fast is enabled, Cucumber
will exit immediately once a scenario fails. The downside of this approach
is that you will lose the opportunity to collect information on any failed
scenarios beyond the first one that failed.

◈ Ruby

You can use fail fast mode by setting the `--fail-fast` command-line flag
when calling `cucumber`.

▣ Java

While CucumberJVM does not have its own fail fast option, the tool
ecosystem used to load and execute CucumberJVM can provide assis-
tance here. There is a configuration option for the Maven Surefire plugin
`skipAfterFailureCount` that allows you to set how many failures can occur
before skipping all remaining tests. Setting this value to "1" is effectively the
same behavior as fail fast. You can set this flag either through the command-
line when calling Maven using `-Dsurefire.skipAfterFailureCount=1` or
through your `./pom.xml` file:

```
<configuration>
    <skipAfterFailureCount>1</skipAfterFailureCount>
</configuration>
```

𝄢 JavaScript

You can also use fail fast mode in CucumberJS by setting the `--fail-fast`
command-line flag when calling `cucumber-js`.

8.3.2 Configurable Fail Fast

There may be cases where you would like to capture failure data on more
than one failed scenario, but still want a performance improvement. A
simple way of collecting more data is increasing the number of scenarios
that can fail before you stop executing tests. As with all of these approaches
there is a trade-off: a higher threshold allows you to collect more data, but
will also increase the duration of your tests in the event of failures.

</> Example #27: Configurable Fail Fast Implementation with Hooks

◇ Ruby

You can use hooks to check the result after each scenario is executed and
then skip any remaining tests if the threshold is reached.

```ruby
# skip all remaining tests once this number has been reached.
$FAILURE_THRESHOLD = 3

# a place to track the number of failed scenario\index{scenario}s.
$failCount = 0

# check if the fail count has been exceeded.
Before do
    skip_this_scenario if $failCount >= $FAILURE_THRESHOLD
end

# increments fail count if the test failed.
After do |scenario|
    $failCount += 1 if scenario.failed?
end
```

⚠ **Pitfall:** In the above example you may have noticed that `$failCount`
is a state value that is shared between scenarios that would seem to violate
a previously stated **Pitfall** in **Chapter 6**. In this case, the sharing of state
across scenarios is necessary and intentional because we are implementing a
test-wide piece of functionality; therefore, the coupling is expected. This
approach can be **very dangerous** because you are potentially affecting the
underlying behavior of your entire test suite, so be mindful of the risks of
such a design when using these techniques to improve performance.

⊟ Java

Usually the Java examples in this book tend to be longer than the
Ruby or JavaScript equivalents. In this case, you can simply set the
`skipAfterFailureCount` configuration option to a value larger than "1" if
you're using the Maven Surefire plugin as shown in the previous example.
We will be building a custom solution for CucumberJVM using hooks in a
later example.

📜 **JavaScript**

You can also use hooks with CucumberJS to check the result after each scenario is executed and then skip any remaining tests if the threshold is reached.

```javascript
const { Before, After } = require('@cucumber/cucumber');

// skip all remaining tests once this number has been reached.
const FAILURE_THRESHOLD = 3;

// a place to track the number of failed scenario\index{scenario}s.
let failCount = 0;

// check if the fail count has been exceeded.
Before(function ({ pickle }) {
    if (failCount >= FAILURE_THRESHOLD) {
        return 'skipped';
    }
});

// increments fail count if the test failed.
After(function ({ pickle, result }) {
    console.log(result);
    if (result.status.toLowerCase() === 'failed') {
        failCount += 1;
    }
});
```

⚠️ **Pitfall:** This example has the same sharing of state between scenarios as the Ruby version of this code, and the same warnings and caveats apply in JavaScript as well.

🏅 **Pro Tip:** There is no "correct" answer for balancing performance with capturing test data. Instead, you should be reviewing your performance and failure data on a regular basis and making adjustments as needed. Also consider adding a parameter to your CI/CD pipeline which allows you to turn fail fast on or off in case you need to collect more failure data. For more information on CI/CD pipelines, refer to **Chapter 9**.

8.3.3 Targeted Fail Fast

A more refined approach is to use scenario tags to target specific categories of scenarios with specific fail fast requirements. For example, you may want to immediately fail the test run if any of the smoke tests fail, but set a higher threshold for other tests. There are a lot of ways to categorize tests, so consider what makes sense for your application as you find the right balance between minimizing test duration and collecting useful failure data.

We will continue to extend our custom hooks from the previous section and introduce a hook implementation of fail fast for Java. As with the other examples in this book, these designs are intended as a starting place for your tests, so feel free to take what is written here and extend it for your application's needs.

</> **Example #28:** Targeted Fail Fast Implementation with Hooks

This example assumes scenario tags in the format **@feature_<number>**.

◇ Ruby

We can extend the previous Ruby example and create an object that tracks failure counts per feature tag.

```ruby
# a place to track the number of failed scenario\index{scenario}s.
$failedFilters = {}
$FAILURE_THRESHOLD = 1

def get_tag_filter(scenario)
    scenario.source_tag_names.filter { |tag| tag.index('@feature_').zero? }.first
end

# check if the fail count has been exceeded.
Before do |scenario|
    filter = get_tag_filter(scenario)
    skip_this_scenario if $failedFilters.key?(filter) &&
                          $failedFilters[filter] >= $FAILURE_THRESHOLD
end

# increments fail count if the test failed.
After do |scenario|
    if scenario.failed?
        filter = get_tag_filter(scenario)
        $failedFilters[filter] = ($failedFilters[filter] || 0) + 1
    end
end
```

🗗 Java

You can implement the same pattern of hooks for CucumberJVM:

```java
public class Hooks {
    private static Map<String, Integer> failedFilters = new Map<String, Integer>();
    private static final int THRESHOLD = 1;

    private String getTagFilter(Scenario scenario) {
        return scenario.getSourceTagNames().stream()
            .filter(tag -> tag.indexOf("@feature_") == 0).findFirst().orElse(null);
    }

    @Before
    public void checkIfSkip(Scenario scenario) {
        String f = getTagFilter(scenario);
        if (failedFilters.containsKey(f) && failedFilters.get(f) >= THRESHOLD) {
            Assumptions.assumeTrue(false); // For JUnit 4 use Assume.assumeTrue
        }
    }

    @After
    public void checkTestResult(Scenario scenario) {
        if (scenario.isFailed()) {
            String f = getTagFilter(scenario);
            failedFilters.put(f,
                (failedFilters.containsKey(f) ? failedFilters.get(f) : 0) + 1);
        }
    }
}
```

⚠ **Pitfall:** This example has the same sharing of state between scenarios as the Ruby and JavaScript versions of this code and the same warnings and caveats apply in Java as well.

📜 **JavaScript**

We can also extend the previous JavaScript example and create an object that tracks failure counts per feature tag.

```javascript
const { Before, After } = require('@cucumber/cucumber');

// a place to track all of the failed scenario\index{scenario}s.
const failedFilters = {};
const FAILURE_THRESHOLD = 1;

// identifies the feature tag using the pickle object.
function getTagFilter(pickle) {
    return pickle.tags.find(i => i.name.indexOf('@feature_') === 0)?.name;
}

// determines if the feature has failed, if it has then skip this test.
Before(function ({ pickle }) {
    const filter = getTagFilter(pickle);
    if (failedFilters[filter] && failedFilters[filter] >= FAILURE_THRESHOLD) {
        return 'skipped';
    }
});

// if a test has failed, record that this feature has also failed.
After(function ({ pickle, result }) {
    const filter = getTagFilter(pickle);
    if (result.status.toLowerCase() === 'failed') {
        failedFilters[filter] = (failedFilters[filter] ?? 0) + 1;
    }
});
```

8.3.4 Targeted Testing with Tag Expressions

Besides improving the performance of your test suite in the event of a failure, you can also reduce test duration by targeting a specific subset of tests to be executed. Unlike fail fast where the trade-off is performance versus data collection, your decisions regarding which tests need to be run for a given circumstance can significantly affect the validity of your tests and impact the quality of your application. Review the special scenario tags and test types that were identified in **Chapter 4** and then decide on appropriate tag expressions to target the test types that your testing needs to support.

For Ruby and JavaScript, you can use the -t "<exp>" or --tags "<exp>" command-line parameters to specify tag expressions. In Java, you can use the -Dcucumber.filter.tags="<exp>" command-line parameter.

🏅 **Pro Tip:** Consider organizing your tag expressions and other command-line parameters using Cucumber profiles. For more information, refer to **Chapter 10**.

8.3.5 Advanced Targeted Testing

If you're using a CI/CD pipeline, tests are run every time a change is made to the source code of your application. For smaller or more monolithic applications, this approach is straightforward. However, when testing applications using a microservice architecture, running all the tests every time a change is made somewhere across hundreds of repositories is not viable, and determining which tests to run is complex and ever-changing. For example, a BFF service depends on one or more microservice APIs, and each one of those APIs depends on others and so on. Additionally, every time microservices are added or modified, so are the relationships between them. How do you decide which tests to run while maintaining quality?

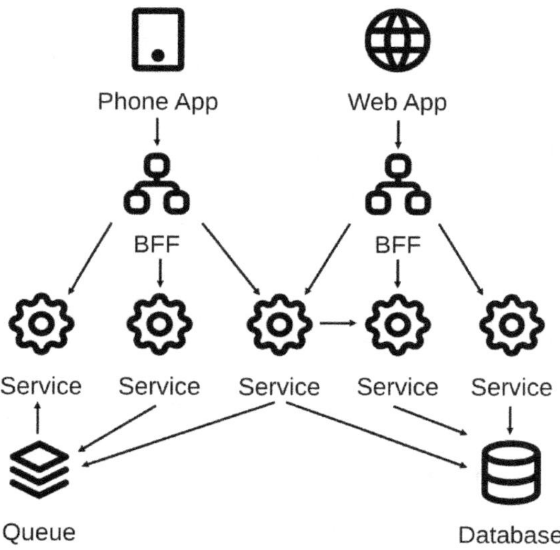

Figure 4: An example of a microservice architecture.

Before deciding which tests need to be run, there are several key pieces of information that need to be collected:

- Which component(s) have changes that require testing
- A dependency graph of all components in the application
- Where the required test suites are located

Supporting test automation for more complex applications such as the example above requires the use of CI/CD and DevOps infrastructure. We'll revisit this example in **Chapter 9** after reviewing how to install and configure the required tools.

8.4 Capturing Performance Metrics

To further optimize the performance of your step definitions and scenarios,
we need to collect performance metrics. Fortunately, Cucumber offers a
standard set of report formatters that can be used to capture additional
information from your test runs.

8.4.1 Cucumber Formatters

In a previous section, we looked at the **rerun** formatter, which generated
an output file containing information on failing scenarios so that Cucumber
could rerun them for us later. Let's look at some of the other available
formatters:

message   Outputs real-time updates where each line of output is a JSON
object with a status message using the Cucumber messages format.[56]

progress   Outputs a visual progress indicator as scenarios are run.

json   Outputs a JSON file that contains performance metrics and test
status for all steps and scenarios.

pretty   A "pretty" output formatter. Note that this is a separate package
for CucumberJS[57]

html   Outputs an HTML report file.

rerun   Outputs a list of failed scenarios that can be used to rerun failed test
cases later. For more information, refer to **8.1.3 Implementing Scenario
Retries**.

junit   Outputs an XML file that is formatted like a JUnit test report. We
will be using this formatter in a future example to integrate with Jenkins.

🏅 **Pro Tip:** If you want to monitor and analyze your Cucumber tests
as they run, consider using the **message** formatter without specifying an
output file so that the messages will be written to stdout. Then, using a
terminal shell, you can direct stdout into your custom program, which can
perform analysis or transmit the data elsewhere by reading stdin: `cucumber
--format message | my-custom-test-analyzer`. You can also use an
existing JSON processing tool such as jq.[58]

---

[56] https://github.com/cucumber/messages
[57] https://www.npmjs.com/package/@cucumber/pretty-formatter
[58] https://jqlang.github.io/jq/

</> **Example #29:** Running Cucumber Formatters

◇ Ruby

You can use formatters with Cucumber for Ruby with the `--format <name>` or `--f <name>` command-line argument. If you want to write the output of the formatter somewhere other than stdout, add the `--out <file | dir | url>` or `-o <file | dir | url>` argument immediately after your format argument.

⊟ Java

You can use formatters with CucumberJVM with the Maven command-line argument `-Dcucumber.plugin="<name>"` or by using the `@ConfigurationParameter` annotation to specify the formatter as a plugin. If you want to write the output of the formatter somewhere other than stdout, add a colon after the formatter name and specify the file path: `html:report.html`.

⌗ JavaScript

You can use formatters with CucumberJS with the `--format <name>` or `--f <name>` command-line argument. If you want to write the output of the formatter somewhere other than stdout, add a colon after the formatter name and specify the file path: `--format html:report.html`.

8.4.2 Cucumber Reports

If you want to publish your test reports directly to the internet, Cucumber reports can be used to automatically push test results to the Cucumber reports website.[59] For Cucumber with Ruby and CucumberJS, you can use the `--publish` flag to publish a Cucumber report. For CucumberJVM you can set `cucumber.publish.enabled=true`.

⚠ **Caution:** Since Cucumber reports are published directly to the internet, do not use this functionality if your team isn't comfortable making your test results publicly available. Keep in mind that a test report may reveal the internal workings of your application, so publishing such data to the internet may not be appropriate for your application.

🏅 **Pro Tip:** The newer versions of Cucumber generate additional output on the screen that advertises Cucumber reports. If you don't want to see these messages, you can set the `CUCUMBER_PUBLISH_QUIET` environment variable to **true** in your current terminal session or globally on your machine.

---

[59] https://reports.cucumber.io/

Chapter 9: Integrating DevOps Infrastructure

Now that we've reviewed the capabilities of Cucumber and Gherkin, it's time to take your automated tests to the next level and integrate them with DevOps infrastructure. Let's take a look at some different types of DevOps tools relevant to running Cucumber.

9.1 Common DevOps Systems

The following directions assume that you are using `bash`[60] as your terminal shell. If you're running these examples on Windows, you may experience issues with file paths. In those cases, use the Windows-formatted path `C:\Users\...` wrapped in double quotes instead.

9.1.1 Package Repositories

Once your CI/CD process successfully creates and validates a build, you will want to store those generated builds somewhere. You may also have a step library and other custom packages and libraries that need to be stored. While there are publicly hosted RubyGems, Maven, and NPM repositories, you may also want to run your own internal package repositories. If your builds generate Docker images, you may also want to host an internal Docker repository as well. Popular products that support all of these package types include Sonatype Nexus, JFrog Artifactory, and Inedo ProGet. You can also archive them as build artifacts within Jenkins.

🏅 **Pro Tip:** Install NPM packages directly through Git if you want to use internal NPM packages without running an NPM package repository by adding an entry to your `./package.json` file in the `dependencies` object: `"repo": "git://github.com/user/repo.git"`

9.1.2 Software Containers

We will be using Docker,[61] a popular software container tool, to install and run the following examples. While originally a Linux program, there are now versions available on all platforms. Software containers provide a standardized way of packaging, shipping, and deploying software applications along with their required dependencies. If you're running many Docker containers in multiple environments, consider using a management tool like Kubernetes[62] to automate complex tasks such as managing pods and scaling out containers.

Run `docker network create devops` to set up a network for your containers before running any of the following Docker examples.

---

[60] https://www.gnu.org/software/bash/
[61] https://www.docker.com/
[62] https://kubernetes.io/

9.1.3 Source Control Systems

Any modern software development organization must have a source control system of some kind. The most popular source control tool is Git,[63] with other options including Mercurial[64] and Subversion.[65] You typically run a client on your machine with a separate server application running either on your local network or on the internet. Hosted Git solutions include GitHub, GitLab, and BitBucket.

If you want to get started with a local Git server, you can use the `git-server` Docker image.[66] Create an SSH key and set up Docker:

```
ssh-keygen -f $HOME/.ssh/id_git
```

```
docker run -d --name git-server --network devops \
  -v git-repositories:/srv/git \
  -v $HOME/.ssh/id_git.pub:/home/git/.ssh/authorized_keys \
  -p 2222:22 \
  --env SSH_AUTH_METHODS=publickey \
  rockstorm/git-server
```

Create or append to file `$HOME/.ssh/config`:

```
Host git-server
    HostName localhost
    User git
    Port 2222
    IdentityFile ~/.ssh/id_git
```

To create a new repository on your server, use SSH to connect:

```
ssh git-server
```

```
mkdir /srv/git/your-project.git
git-init --bare /srv/git/your-project.git
```

You can access your repositories by running this command:

```
git clone ssh://git-server/srv/git/your-project.git
```

For more information, refer to the documentation for `git-server`. If you are experiencing errors when logging in with a public key:

```
docker exec -it git-server sh
/ # chmod go-w /home/git
/ # chmod 700 /home/git/.ssh
/ # chmod 600 /home/git/.ssh/authorized_keys
```

[63] https://git-scm.com/

[64] https://www.mercurial-scm.org/

[65] https://subversion.apache.org/

[66] https://github.com/rockstorm101/git-server-docker

9.1.4 Build Systems

When changes are made to your application's source code, the build system
is notified and runs the build process on that application. Once built, your
test automation should be executed against that application to ensure that
all functional tests are passing. Popular build systems include Jenkins and
TeamCity as well as built-in ones for GitHub and GitLab.

If you want to get started with a local Jenkins server, you can use the
`jenkins/jenkins` Docker image[67] and run builds through it:

```
docker run -d --name jenkins-server --network devops \
  -v jenkins_home:/var/jenkins_home \
  -p 8081:8080 -p 50000:50000 \
  jenkins/jenkins:lts
```

After starting the docker container, look for the setup password to be written
to the Docker logs. You can now browse to `http://localhost:8081`, enter
the password to initialize your instance, and install the default plugins. For
more information, refer to the documentation for `jenkins/jenkins`.

9.1.5 Issue Tracking Tools

As a software project is updated, it is important to track the work items
being completed and to associate those tasks with automated tests so that
you can answer the question "Is requirement x currently passing or failing?"
Popular internet-based issue tracking tools include Jira,[68] Rally,[69] and
Trello.[70] There are also open-source and self-hosted alternatives such as
OpenProject.[71]

If you want to get started with a local OpenProject server, you can use the
`openproject/community` Docker image:[72]

```
docker run -d --name openproject --network devops -p 8082:80 \
  -e OPENPROJECT_SECRET_KEY_BASE=secret \
  -e OPENPROJECT_HOST__NAME=localhost:8082 \
  -e OPENPROJECT_HTTPS=false \
  -e OPENPROJECT_DEFAULT__LANGUAGE=en \
  openproject/community:13
```

You can now browse to `http://localhost:8082` and enter the default
username/password `admin admin` to get started. For more information,
refer to the documentation for `openproject/community`.

---

[67] https://hub.docker.com/r/jenkins/jenkins
[68] https://www.atlassian.com/software/jira
[69] https://www.broadcom.com/products/software/value-stream-management/rally
[70] https://trello.com/
[71] https://www.openproject.org/community-edition/
[72] https://www.openproject.org/docs/installation-and-operations/installation/docker/

9.1.6 Monitoring Tools

There may be additional data that you collect as part of your testing such
as logging and performance data, which can prove useful to improving
the quality of your tests and your software. Capturing and storing this
information for reporting can be an important source of feedback for the
team. Popular tools for storing this information include DynaTrace, Azure
Monitor, and Datadog. There are also popular open-source alternatives
such as Graylog and Splunk.

If you want to get started with a local Graylog server, you can use the
`graylog` Docker image:[73]

```
docker run -d --name mongodb --network devops \
  mongo:3

docker run -d --name elasticsearch --network devops \
  -e "http.host=0.0.0.0" \
  -e "ES_JAVA_OPTS=-Xms512m -Xmx512m" \
  docker.elastic.co/elasticsearch/elasticsearch-oss:6.8.5

docker run -d --name graylog --network devops \
  -p 9000:9000 -p 12201:12201 -p 1514:1514 \
  -e GRAYLOG_HTTP_EXTERNAL_URI="http://127.0.0.1:9000/" \
  graylog/graylog:3.2
```

You can now browse to `http://localhost:9000` and enter the default
username/password `admin admin` to get started. For more information,
refer to the documentation for `graylog`.

9.1.7 Test Reporting Tools

If you want to have a more QA-focused tool for monitoring and analyzing
test results, you can use Report Portal for storing and reporting on them
from your CI/CD builds. To get started, use the `reportportal` Docker
images:[74]

```
URL=https://raw.githubusercontent.com/reportportal/reportportal
curl -LO $URL/master/docker-compose.yml
export RP_INITIAL_ADMIN_PASSWORD=******
docker-compose -p reportportal up -d --force-recreate
```

You can now browse to `http://localhost:8080` and login. For more
information, refer to the Report Portal Installation Guide.[75]

---

[73] https://archivedocs.graylog.org/en/latest/pages/installation/docker.html
[74] https://hub.docker.com/u/reportportal/
[75] https://reportportal.io/installation

9.2 CI/CD and DevOps

Let's talk more about the relationship between DevOps and CI/CD and how these processes can help improve the quality of software.

One of the primary objectives of DevOps is to automate the process of building, deploying, and maintaining software so that these processes can be more predictable and less prone to human error. continuous integration allows for automating software builds and continuous delivery supports automated deployments, so CI/CD is a major component of any DevOps implementation.

In order to improve the process of building software and to enable more automated maintenance of software, we'll need to introduce some new concepts. Let's talk about shift left and shift right and why you will want to incorporate both of these approaches into your DevOps processes.

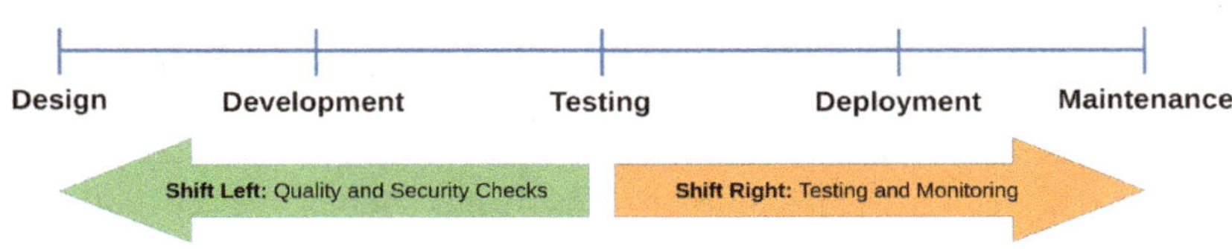

Figure 5: Shift Left and Shift Right

9.2.1 Shift Left

If you've ever experienced the impact caused by a bug in a production software system, then you know that it's a lot easier to fix problems if you catch them earlier in the software development process. The goal of "shift left" is to identify security and quality issues with software as soon as possible. Using automated CI/CD pipelines is a critical component of this strategy since it allows automatic test runs to be initiated as soon as source code changes. Preventing failures from reaching your production systems will improve the quality of your software, reduce the amount of time your team has to spend in panic mode, and generally improve your team's performance and well-being.

9.2.2 Shift Right

While performing testing earlier in your software development process will reduce defects, problems are bound to occur in the testing and production environments. In these cases, you'll need to have a way to validate that the production environment is behaving as expected and be notified the moment something unexpected happens. The goal of "shift right" is to collect important metrics about the test and production environments in order to inform decisions made earlier in the software development process. In an earlier chapter, we talked about smoke testing and the ability to run smoke tests in the test and production environments; this is an example of shift right.

For a more in-depth dive into DevOps and how to apply these concepts at scale, refer to **Further Reading**.

9.2.3 Continuous Processes

So far, we've talked a lot about CI/CD pipelines and why you want to have them as part of your software development process. Something to keep in mind is that both C's in CI/CD stand for *Continuous*, which is important to consider. Any effective DevOps process is continuous: by definition, it never ends. One of the core concepts of agile methodology is that software is never completed, so it makes sense that neither are the processes by which software is built, tested, deployed, and maintained.

9.3 Running Tests with a Jenkins CI/CD Pipeline

Let's go ahead and take all the tools we've looked at so far, from Cucumber to CI/CD and DevOps infrastructure, and put them together into a working build and test process. There are different stages within the pipeline that support building, testing, and deploying your application:

First, a change in your Git repository triggers a build in Jenkins.

1) **Checkout**: Pulls down the latest code from Git.
2) **Build**: Performs a build on the application's source code to verify that it compiles before running tests.

🏅 **Pro Tip:** If your Cucumber tests perform integration testing or end-to-end testing, you may need to deploy your application before running your Cucumber tests, which means you would have a **Unit Testing** stage, then a **Deployment** stage, and finally a **Test** stage for Cucumber.

3) **Test**:

    1) Generates a test configuration file based on the current environment. If you have secrets and passwords, utilize a key vault program or one of many Jenkins plugins designed to assist with this process. **Do not commit secrets and passwords to source control.**

    2) Runs your tests. Consider adding a formatter to capture test results so you can report them to Jenkins later.

    3) Reports the test results to Jenkins. You will still get pass/fail without this extra step because Jenkins will interpret a non-zero program exit code as a build failure; however, you should write the test report details to Jenkins so you can capture data about the individual tests that failed.

4) **Publish/Deploy**: Captures your build artifacts (compiled executables, transpiled files, etc.) and stores them. You can push them to a package repository, archive them in Jenkins, or zip and copy them to a file server.

5) **Promote**: The final step of the pipeline is promoting the build to the next CI/CD pipeline such as a staging environment. In a fully automated CI/CD pipeline, code changes merged into the "development" branch are tested and promoted to a staging environment where automated acceptance testing is performed, and finally, the changes are automatically deployed to production. You can also add manual gates between promotion environments if your software requires customer or management sign-off before proceeding.

</> Example #30: A CI/CD Pipeline From Start to Finish

This example assumes that you have both the git-server and jenkins-server Docker containers running on your local machine, and that you have configured them according to the installation directions at the beginning of this chapter.

9.3.1 Setting Up Git

1) In a terminal, run **ssh git-server** to connect to the Git server.

2) Once connected, run the following commands:

```
mkdir /srv/git/rubyproject1.git
mkdir /srv/git/javaproject1.git
mkdir /srv/git/nodeproject1.git
git-init --bare /srv/git/rubyproject1.git
git-init --bare /srv/git/javaproject1.git
git-init --bare /srv/git/nodeproject1.git
```

3) In a directory where you want to keep your code locally, run:

```
git clone ssh://git-server/srv/git/rubyproject1.git
git clone ssh://git-server/srv/git/javaproject1.git
git clone ssh://git-server/srv/git/nodeproject1.git
```

4) Set up each project according to the installation instructions from **Chapter 5** for each respective language.

9.3.2 Setting up Jenkins

1) In a terminal, run the following command:

```
docker exec -it --user root jenkins-server bash
```

2) After connecting to the container, run the following commands:

```
curl -sL https://deb.nodesource.com/setup_20.x | bash -
apt-get install nodejs -y
apt-get install ruby ruby-dev libgmp3-dev build-essential -y
gem install cucumber
MVN_BIN=https://dlcdn.apache.org/maven/maven-3/3.9.6/binaries
curl -O $MVN_BIN/apache-maven-3.9.6-bin.tar.gz
tar -xvf apache-maven-3.9.6-bin.tar.gz
mv apache-maven-3.9.6 /opt/
```

⚠ **Pitfall:** Do not run Jenkins agents directly on the main instance in a production environment. This is a sandbox environment that allows you to see the entire process of running a CI/CD pipeline on your local machine.

3) Open the Jenkins UI through a browser at `http://localhost:8081` and log in.

4) Under "Manage Jenkins" > "Security" menu item, go to "Git Host Key Verification" and set it to the "accept first connection" option.

5) For each Git repository:

   1) Click on + `New Item`

   2) Select `Multi-branch Pipeline`

   3) Set the name and description.

   4) Select the "git" provider and type:

      `ssh://git-server/srv/git/repo.git`

   5) Select the existing "git" credential, or add a new Jenkins credential provider credential and select "ssh username with private key." Use "git" as username and paste the contents of the private key file `~/.ssh/id_git` that you generated earlier. Add the passcode if you chose to have a passcode.

   6) Set "scan multibranch pipeline triggers" to interval 1 minute.

⚠ **Caution:** In a larger CI/CD installation, you should use webhooks to push source control change notifications to Jenkins instead of having Jenkins scan the Git repositories periodically. GitHub, GitLab, and other source control management tools can be configured to do this. As mentioned before, this approach is designed to simplify creating a local sandbox CI/CD.

9.3.3 Programming a Jenkins Pipeline

Since Jenkins itself is built on Java, pipelines are written using a Jenkins-flavored version of Groovy, which is a scripting language designed to run on JVM so it's compatible with Java libraries and tools. Let's review some components of the pipeline file:

- `node` - Informs Jenkins that your pipeline needs a machine to run on.
- `checkout scm` - Tells Jenkins to pull the latest code.
- `sh '{command}'` - Executes the specified terminal command.
- `stage('{name}')` - Defines a specific step of your pipeline. Any code within the block will show as running within that stage. When you view the status of a branch in Jenkins, each column in the pipeline view will match each stage that you have defined within the pipeline. This is helpful for identifying pass/fail of each step of the build as well as being able to review performance metrics.

Running Cucumber for Ruby on Jenkins requires a few steps. Since you already installed `ruby`, `ruby-devel`, and `cucumber` on the jenkins-server Docker container, you can access those applications from within your pipeline.

Let's make a few modifications to the test project first. Add a new build target to the `Rakefile`:

```ruby
Cucumber::Rake::Task.new(:ci) do |t|
    t.cucumber_opts = [
        '--publish-quiet', '--strict', '--format progress'
    ]
end
```

Also go ahead and create a feature file and a step definition or two if you wish. Finally, create a file in the top-level directory of your "rubyproject1" repository called `Jenkinsfile`:

```groovy
node {
    stage('Checkout') {
        checkout scm
    }

    stage('Build') {
        echo 'Build your ruby application...'
    }

    stage('Test') {
        sh 'rake ci'
    }

    stage('Deploy') { echo 'Deploying!' }

    stage('Promote') { echo 'Promote!' }
}
```

After creating this file, use Git to push your changes back to `git-server`. When you open Jenkins, you should see a build initiate automatically within one minute. You should also see each of your stages running and showing green as they pass.

Pro Tip: Avoid writing code directly in your `Jenkinsfile` and instead use a Jenkins Shared Library[76] for managing common functions. For more information, refer to **9.6 Using Jenkins Shared Libraries.**

---

[76]https://www.jenkins.io/doc/book/pipeline/shared-libraries/

▤ Java

Running CucumberJVM on Jenkins is a similar process to the other variants
of Cucumber. You already installed Maven on the jenkins-server Docker
container, so you will use Maven to execute the tests during the build. First,
configure a Maven profile in your `pom.xml` by adding to `project/profiles`:

```xml
<profile>
  <id>profile-ci</id>
  <build>
    <plugins>
      <plugin>
        <groupId>org.apache.maven.plugins</groupId>
        <artifactId>maven-surefire-plugin</artifactId>
        <configuration>
          <properties>
            <configurationParameters>
              cucumber.plugin=progress,junit:build/reports/output.xml
              cucumber.publish.quiet=true
            </configurationParameters>
          </properties>
        </configuration>
      </plugin>
    </plugins>
  </build>
</profile>
```

For more information about Maven profiles, refer to **10.1.2**. Next,
update the `RunCucumberTest.java` file to remove the annotation
`@ConfigurationParameter` with key `PLUGIN_PROPERTY_NAME`. If this
parameter is set within this file, Maven profiles will not be able to override
it. Now, go ahead and create a `Jenkinsfile`:

```groovy
node {
    stage('Checkout') {
        checkout scm
    }

    stage('Build') {
        echo 'Build your java application...'
    }

    stage('Test') {
        sh '''
        M2_HOME='/opt/apache-maven-3.9.6'
        PATH="$M2_HOME/bin:$PATH"
        mvn test -Pprofile-ci
        '''
    }

    stage('Deploy') { echo 'Deploying!' }

    stage('Promote') { echo 'Promote!' }
}
```

After creating this file, use Git to push your changes back to `git-server`.
When you open Jenkins, you should see a build initiate automatically within
one minute. You should also see each of your stages running and showing
green as they pass.

📜 **JavaScript**

Using CucumberJS with Jenkins is also very similar to the way you integrated Cucumber for Ruby. To get started, update the `package.json` with a new run script called "ci-test":

```
{
  "scripts": {
    "test": "cucumber-js",
    "ci-test": "cucumber-js --strict -f progress"
  }
}
```

Now let's create a `Jenkinsfile`:

```
node {
    stage('Checkout') {
        checkout scm
    }

    stage('Build') {
        echo 'Build your nodejs application...'
    }

    stage('Test') {
        sh 'npm run ci-test'
    }

    stage('Deploy') { echo 'Deploying!' }

    stage('Promote') { echo 'Promote!' }
}
```

After creating this file, use Git to push your changes back to `git-server`. When you open Jenkins, you should see a build initiate automatically within one minute. You should also see each of your stages running and showing green as they pass.

🎖 **Pro Tip:** When running scenarios through CI/CD pipelines, always use strict mode so that undefined or pending steps cause the build to fail. To use strict mode, use the `--strict` flag for Cucumber for Ruby and CucumberJS. As of CucumberJVM 7, strict mode is the only option and the ability to turn it on and off has been removed. In older versions, the `strict` Cucumber option was available.

While this example allows for pass/fail of a build to be tracked and recorded by Jenkins, in the next section you will add a formatter to capture all the test run data so that Jenkins can provide you with more useful analysis.

9.4 Integrating Test Reporting

Now that you can run your test automation as part of a CI/CD pipeline, you will want to capture and store additional metrics about your tests such as how long they take to run and which scenarios and steps are failing.

</> Example #31: Collecting Test Metrics with Jenkins

One of the default plugins installed in Jenkins is the JUnit plugin. This plugin can read and process JUnit test report XML files. Since Cucumber has a formatter that can generate test reports in this format, you can easily connect Cucumber with Jenkins test reporting.

Pro Tip: Consider installing additional Jenkins plugins such as Test Results Analyzer[77] for enhanced reporting capabilities.

To begin, let's return to the previous example from **9.4 Running Tests with a CI/CD Pipeline** and make some modifications.

Ruby

In the "rubyproject1" directory, modify "ci" in your `rakefile`:

```ruby
Cucumber::Rake::Task.new(:ci) do |t|
    t.cucumber_opts = [
        '--publish-quiet', '--strict', '--format progress',
        '--format junit', '--out build/reports'
    ]
end
```

In the `Jenkinsfile`, update the "Test" stage:

```groovy
stage('Test') {
    try {
        sh 'npm run ci-test'
    } finally { junit 'build/reports/**/*.xml' }
}
```

After committing and pushing these changes to Git, a new build in Jenkins should initiate. After the build runs, you should be able to see the JUnit test report by clicking "Test Result" when you navigate to the specific build number in your branch.

Java

In the "javaproject1" directory, update "profile-ci" in your `pom.xml`:

```xml
<configurationParameters>
    cucumber.plugin=progress,junit:build/reports/output.xml
    cucumber.publish.quiet=true
</configurationParameters>
```

---

[77] https://plugins.jenkins.io/test-results-analyzer/

In the `Jenkinsfile`, update the "Test" stage:

```
stage('Test') {
    try {
        sh '''
        M2_HOME='/opt/apache-maven-3.9.6'
        PATH="$M2_HOME/bin:$PATH"
        mvn test -Pprofile-ci
        '''
    } finally { junit 'build/reports/**/*.xml' }
}
```

After committing and pushing these changes to Git, a new build in Jenkins should initiate. After the build runs, you should be able to see the JUnit test report by clicking "Test Result" when you navigate to the specific build number in your branch.

JavaScript

In the "nodeproject1" directory, update the run scripts in `package.json`:

```
{
  "scripts": {
    "test": "cucumber-js",
    "ci-test": "cucumber-js --strict -f progress -f junit:build/reports/output.xml"
  }
}
```

In the `Jenkinsfile`, update the "Test" stage:

```
stage('Test') {
    try {
        sh 'npm run ci-test'
    } finally { junit 'build/reports/**/*.xml' }
}
```

After committing and pushing these changes to Git, a new build in Jenkins should initiate. After the build runs, you should be able to see the JUnit test report by clicking "Test Result" when you navigate to the specific build number in your branch.

Pro Tip: Use the Cucumber `json` formatter to generate a JSON test report, then use jq[78] to determine pass/fail data by user story:

```
jq -r '.[].elements[] | select(.tags[] | .name | startswith("@story-")) as $ex |
"\($ex.tags[0].name): \($ex.steps[-1]?.result.status // "UNKNOWN")"' report.json
```

This script assumes that your user story scenario tags are in the format `@story-<number>`. You can then send the results to Jira, Rally, etc.

---

[78] https://jqlang.github.io/jq/

9.5 Test Targeting With CI/CD

In a previous section, we looked at the challenges related to improving performance while testing in a microservice architecture. Now that you've had some experience implementing a basic CI/CD pipeline in Jenkins, let's revisit these challenges and consider some possible solutions.

9.5.1 Setting Default Tag Expressions

When running tests in Jenkins, you may wish to have some basic test filters in place to run more targeted testing.

</> Example #32: Setting Tag Expressions for CI/CD

◇ Ruby

In the previous examples, you used **rake** to manage the different options. Let's use profiles instead. Start by creating a file **cucumber.yml**:

```
default: -f pretty
ci: --publish-quiet --strict -f progress -f junit --out build/reports -t "not @wip"
```

You'll also need to change the **rakefile** file to use the new profiles:

```
Cucumber::Rake::Task.new(:features) do |t|
    t.cucumber_opts = [] # the "default" profile will be used if none is specified.
end

Cucumber::Rake::Task.new(:ci) do |t|
    t.cucumber_opts = ['-p ci']
end
```

▤ Java

In order to be able to use tag expressions through CucumberJVM and Maven, some additional setup in your Maven profile is required:

```
<properties>
    <cucumber.filter.tags>not @wip</cucumber.filter.tags>
</properties>
<build>
    <plugins>
        <plugin>
            <groupId>org.apache.maven.plugins</groupId>
            <artifactId>maven-surefire-plugin</artifactId>
            <configuration><properties>
                <configurationParameters>
                    cucumber.plugin=progress,junit:build/reports/output.xml
                    cucumber.publish.quiet=true
                    cucumber.filter.tags=${cucumber.filter.tags}
                </configurationParameters>
            </properties></configuration>
        </plugin>
    </plugins>
</build>
```

📜 JavaScript

As with Ruby, let's go ahead and set up Cucumber profiles for CucumberJS. Start by creating a file `./cucumber.js`:

```javascript
module.exports = {
    'default': {},
    'ci': {
        format: ['progress', 'junit:build/reports/output.xml'],
        strict: true,
        tags: 'not @wip'
    }
};
```

You'll also need to change the **package.json** file to use the new profiles:

```json
{
  "scripts": {
    "test": "cucumber-js",
    "ci-test": "cucumber-js -p ci"
  }
}
```

9.5.2 Targeting Tag Expressions at Build Time

In more complex application testing situations such as when working with microservices, you may want to decide which subset of tests to execute from within Jenkins and then ask Cucumber to execute that subset. Let's look at how to use tag expressions through the command-line to add an expression that runs `@regression` tests as well as continuing to ignore `@wip`.

💎 Ruby

```
cucumber -p ci -t @regression
```

☕ Java

```
mvn test -Pprofile-ci \
  -Dcucumber.filter.tags="not @wip and @regression"
```

⚠️ **Pitfall:** Unlike Ruby and JavaScript, the tag parameter in Cucumber-JVM and Maven replaces the previous default value and isn't cumulative.

📜 JavaScript

```
npm run ci -- -t @regression
```

You can replace the call to run the tests in your **Jenkinsfile** with the above examples and the additional filtering will apply when Jenkins runs the build.

Now that you can pass tag expressions at build time into Cucumber, how can Jenkins determine which tests need to run?

9.5.3 Collecting Dependency Information

Since CI/CD pipelines in Jenkins are built using Groovy, you can perform HTTP calls, database lookups, or any other types of calls to systems you need information from in order to decide which tests need to run. For example, if you had a microservice called `service-2` that was called by `service-1` and `service-3` as well as `bff-1` and `bff-2`, then you would want to run regression testing on those other services to confirm that code changes to `service-2` have not broken any dependent services.

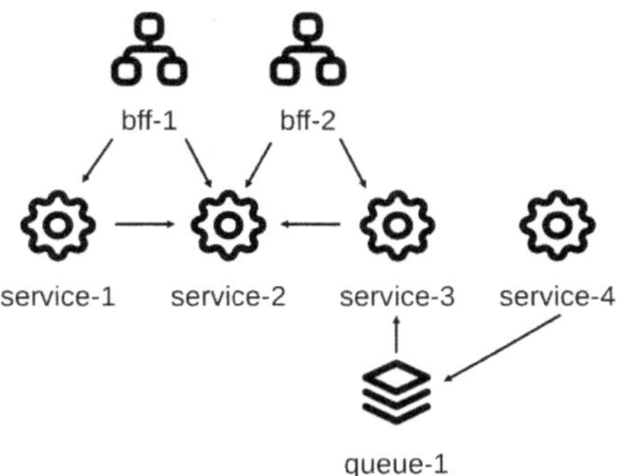

Figure 6: A hypothetical microservice architecture.

Typically, the relationships between components in a microservice architecture can be determined by inspecting configuration files. Suppose the following YAML configuration file exists for each microservice:

```
name: service name
services:
    - service that can be called.
queues:
    send:
        - queues that can be sent to.
    receive:
        - queues that can be received from.
```

If you were to acquire the configuration files for all services in this application, it would be possible to construct a dependency graph to identify which services depended on which other services. If service A directly calls (through HTTP, RPC, etc.) service B or sends a message to a queue expecting service B to receive it, then service A depends on B. To answer the question of which tests need to be run, you first need to generate a list of components that depend on the component that changed.

</> Example #33: Building a Simple Dependency Graph

Let's take a look at a simple implementation for a dependency graph built in Groovy that stores relationships using a `Map`:

 **Groovy**

```groovy
def map = [:]

def addDependency(Map<String, String[]> map, String item, String dependentItem) {
    if (map.containsKey(dependentItem)) {
        map[dependentItem] << item
    } else {
        map[dependentItem] = [item]
    }
}

def getDependents(Map<String, String[]> map, String item, int levels) {
    if (levels <= 0 || !map.containsKey(item)) {
        return []
    }

    def dependents = []
    map[item]?.each { dependent ->
        dependents << dependent
        dependents += getDependents(map, dependent, levels - 1)
    }
    dependents
}

// example of loading the dependencies from Figure 6:
addDependency(map, 'bff-1', 'service-1')
addDependency(map, 'bff-1', 'service-2')
addDependency(map, 'bff-2', 'service-2')
addDependency(map, 'bff-2', 'service-3')
addDependency(map, 'service-1', 'service-2')
addDependency(map, 'service-3', 'service-2')
addDependency(map, 'queue-1', 'service-3')
addDependency(map, 'service-4', 'queue-1')
```

Suppose you were to execute the following function call:

```groovy
getDependents(map, 'service-2', 1)
```

The result would be `[bff-1, bff-2, service-1, service-3]`. In many cases, one level of dependents is sufficient for making decisions about which tests to run. However, when services are dependent through intermediary paths such as message queues, you may need to scan two or three levels down the graph. From the prior example, since `service-3` owns a message queue and `service-4` depends on that queue, you would need to look at two levels of dependencies to see the relationship.

Pro Tip: For a more robust implementation of dependency graphs, including support for more complex situations such as dependency cycles, consider using a third-party library like JGraphT.[79]

---

[79] https://jgrapht.org/

9.5.4 Building Tag Expressions Dynamically

Once you have determined which tests to execute based on the changes to your application, you need a way to communicate these to Cucumber. As we have discussed previously, you can use tag expressions to control which tests are run by Cucumber.

</> Example #34: Targeting Tests Dynamically in Jenkins

This example assumes that you have scenarios in different feature files where each scenario is tagged with the components of your microservice architecture being tested by that scenario. For example:

```
@service-1
Scenario: A scenario for service-1
# ...

@service-2
Scenario: A scenario for service-2
# ...

@service-3
Scenario: A scenario for service-3
# ...
```

Let's look at how to build tag expressions dynamically in Jenkins pipelines.

⭐ Groovy

```groovy
def generateTagExpression(List<String> services) {
    services.collect { service -> "@$service" }.join(' or ')
}
```

If you call this function and pass `['service-1','service-2','service-3']`, it will generate the output `@service-1 or @service-2 or @service-3`. You will need to pass the list of dependent services as well as the service that changed to this function to generate the tag expression for Cucumber. Before continuing, let's go ahead and put the direct calls to Cucumber in reusable functions in order to simplify the process of passing tag expressions.

9.5.5 Running Cucumber as a Function

As your Jenkins pipeline code becomes more complex, it is important to stay organized and encapsulate commonly used functionality into reusable functions. The shell code in a Jenkins pipeline in particular can be confusing and messy, and should not be copy/pasted directly. Building sensible functions to manage these critical aspects of the CI/CD pipeline can make maintaining the pipelines easier as your applications grow. In the next section we will also look at how to share these functions across multiple pipelines.

</> Example #35: Using Functions for Running Cucumber

◈ Ruby

```groovy
def executeCucumberRubyTests(options) {
    def tags = options?.tags
    def command = 'cucumber -p ci'
    if (tags != null && tags.length() > 0) { command += " -t \"$tags\"" }
    sh command
}
```

Java

```groovy
def executeCucumberJVMTests(options) {
    def tags = options?.tags
    def command = 'mvn test -Pprofile-ci'
    if (tags != null && tags.length() > 0) {
        command += " -Dcucumber.filter.tags=\"$tags\""
    }
    sh """
M2_HOME='/opt/apache-maven-3.9.6'
PATH="\$M2_HOME/bin:\$PATH"
$command
"""
}
```

JavaScript

```groovy
def executeCucumberJSTests(options) {
    def tags = options?.tags
    def command = 'npm run ci-test'
    if (tags != null && tags.length() > 0) { command += " -t \"$tags\"" }
    sh command
}
```

</> Example #36: Advanced Test Targeting From Start to Finish

Let's use all the code from this section to build a complete example.

★ Groovy

```groovy
def changedService = 'service-2' // determine this based on code changes.
def dependencies = [:] // load these dependencies from your configuration files.

def getServicesRequiringTesting(String changedService, Map dependencies) {
    [changedService] + getDependents(dependencies, changedService)
}

stage('Test') {
    def tags = generateTagExpression(
        getServicesRequiringTesting(changedService, dependencies))
    try {
        executeCucumberRubyTests([ tags: tags ])
    } finally { junit 'build/reports/**/*.xml' }
}
```

9.6 Using Jenkins Shared Libraries

Now that you're starting to build out some functions in Groovy to manage common tasks in Jenkins, you'll want to keep these common functions in a Jenkins Shared Library so that you don't have to copy/paste code.

9.6.1 Setting Up a Shared Library

1) In a terminal, run **ssh git-server** to connect to the Git server.

2) Once connected, run the following commands:

```
mkdir /srv/git/jenkins-common-lib.git
git-init --bare /srv/git/jenkins-common-lib.git
```

3) In a directory where you want to keep your code locally, run:

```
git clone ssh://git-server/srv/git/jenkins-common-lib.git
```

4) Within the **jenkins-shared-lib** directory, create the following:

- **./vars** - this is where your Groovy files will live.
- **./resources** - you can add additional resources files here.

When Jenkins loads a shared library, each of the Groovy files within **./vars** will be available as an object based on the name of the file. For example, if you have a file named **functions.groovy**, it will be accessible within a **Jenkinsfile** as **functions**. You can either define multiple functions within each Groovy file and call them using the name of the file such as **functions.func1()**, or define a function called **call** that can be called directly based on the file name such as **functions()**.

⚠ **Pitfall:** Always use a lowercase letter for the first character for Groovy files in **./vars**. Otherwise, Jenkins may not resolve function names properly. Both Java and JavaScript recommend camel case for function names.

5) Create a new Groovy file called **./vars/tests.groovy**. Now take all the Cucumber-related functions you wrote in the last section and put them together here. Also add this function:

```groovy
def executeCucumberTests(options) {
    def lang = options?.language
    switch (lang) {
        case 'ruby':
            return executeCucumberRubyTests(options)
        case 'java':
            return executeCucumberJVMTests(options)
        case 'javascript':
            return executeCucumberJSTests(options)
    }
    throw new IllegalArgumentException("Unsupported language: $lang")
}
```

⚠ **Caution:** In the previous example, you may have considered using strategy pattern and created a map to track the relationship between the name of the language and each function that runs tests, and then called the appropriate function dynamically at runtime. However, Jenkins performs special processing on Groovy to support custom functionality, so performing dynamic function calls can cause unexpected warnings from Jenkins such as "CPS Method Mismatch".[80]

6) Push your changes to `git-server` and open the Jenkins UI. Navigate to "Manage Jenkins" > "System" menu item. Scroll down to "Global Pipeline Libraries" and Click the "Add" button.

7) Enter "common-lib" for the name of the library. Enter "main" for the default version.

8) Under the "Source Control Management" options, select "git" and type the path: `ssh://git-server/srv/git/jenkins-common-lib.git`. Select your existing Git credential for accessing the library. Finally, click "Save" to complete the process.

9.6.2 Using a Shared Library

The new shared library is now ready to use. To load the library in your `Jenkinsfile`, you simply need to add `library 'common-lib'` at the top of your file. By default, Jenkins will load the default version specified when you configured the shared library in Jenkins. You can also target a specific branch version of a library with `library 'name@version'`.[81]

</> Example #37: Using Shared Library from a Pipeline

Let's modify our existing `Jenkinsfiles` in the local git projects.

 **Ruby**

At the top of the `Jenkinsfile`, add the following line:

```
library 'common-lib'
```

Then, replace the "test" stage with the following:

```
stage('Test') {
    try {
        tests.executeCucumberTests([
            language: 'ruby'
        ])
    } finally { junit 'build/reports/**/*.xml' }
}
```

---

[80] https://www.jenkins.io/doc/book/pipeline/cps-method-mismatches/
[81] https://www.jenkins.io/doc/book/pipeline/shared-libraries/

🔖 Java

The directions are the same for Java except the specified language needs to be `'java'`.

📜 JavaScript

The directions are the same for JavaScript except the specified language needs to be `'javascript'`.

9.6.3 Creating Reusable Pipelines

After the latest changes to your existing Jenkins files, you may have noticed that each of the three pipelines are almost identical. In a large microservice environment with potentially hundreds of pipelines, it would be ideal to automatically generate the pipelines, so any updates to infrastructure do not require making changes to every `Jenkinsfile` in your Git repositories.

</> Example #38: Using a Pipeline Builder Function

Let's use a Jenkins Shared Library to build a function for generating pipelines, and then replace the existing `Jenkinsfile` code with a single function call.

1) Create a file in the `jenkins-common-lib` repository called `./vars/buildPipeline.groovy`:

```groovy
def call(options) {
    def language = options?.language

    node {
        stage('Checkout') {
            checkout scm
        }

        stage('Build') {
            echo "Build your $language application..."
        }

        stage('Test') {
            try {
                tests.executeCucumberTests([
                    language: language
                ])
            } finally { junit 'build/reports/**/*.xml' }
        }

        stage('Deploy') {
            echo 'Deploying!'
        }

        stage('Promote') {
            echo 'Promote!'
        }
    }
}
```

2) Check these changes into `git-server`. Now you can use this function in each of your projects.

3) Finally, update the `Jenkinsfile` for each of your existing pipelines:

💎 Ruby

Navigate to **rubyproject1** repository, and change your `Jenkinsfile`:

```
library 'common-lib'

buildPipeline([
    language: 'ruby'
])
```

☕ Java

Navigate to **javaproject1** repository, and change your `Jenkinsfile`:

```
library 'common-lib'

buildPipeline([
    language: 'java'
])
```

📜 JavaScript

Navigate to **nodeproject1** repository, and change your `Jenkinsfile`:

```
library 'common-lib'

buildPipeline([
    language: 'javascript'
])
```

🏅 **Pro Tip:** Add any additional parameters to `options` such as build environment, test types, tag expressions, etc.

While building your Jenkins CI/CD pipelines dynamically is more complex, it can improve maintainability, especially if there are hundreds of projects that need to be built and tested through your build system.

9.7 Generating Living Documentation

One of the defining features of executable specifications is that your scenarios can serve as human-readable documentation. While reading conventional unit testing code can be helpful for software developers, the readability of feature files for people who understand your application's business rules is crucial to validating that the software being delivered is actually meeting the original needs of the customer.

In some cases, you may also need to provide written documentation to your customers or stakeholders as part of your deliverables to them. While you could simply send them the feature files as is, instead consider using Pickles[82] to convert your specifications into different formats.

9.7.1 Installing Pickles

1) Install Microsoft .NET Framework 6.[83]

2) Download the Pickles[84] zip file based on your OS, then copy the unzipped directory to where you normally store programs.

3) Add the directory to `PATH`, so you can run it through a terminal.

9.7.2 Running Pickles

Now that you've installed the required software to run Pickles, let's generate some documentation. Pickles supports the following formats:

html   Generates a simple static HTML site with pages.

dhtml   Generates a dynamic HTML site with client-side search.

word   Generates a `.docx` file for word processing applications.

excel   Generates a `.xlsx` file for spreadsheet applications.

</> Example #39: Generating a Word Document

In a terminal, navigate to the root directory of one of your Cucumber projects. Then run the following command:

```
pickles -f ./features -o ./docs --df=word
```

You will now have a Word document containing all of your scenarios. Any of the other formatters above can be used with the `--df` flag to change the output format.

---

[82] https://github.com/picklesdoc/pickles
[83] https://dotnet.microsoft.com/en-us/download/dotnet/6.0
[84] https://github.com/picklesdoc/pickles/releases

9.7.3 Integrating Pickles with CI/CD

Now that you can generate documentation from your feature files, consider running Pickles as part of your CI/CD pipeline so that the process of generating the documentation is completely automated.

Setting Up Jenkins

1) In a terminal, run the following command:

```
docker exec -it --user root jenkins-server bash
```

2) After connecting to the container, run the following commands:

```
cd ~
URL=https://packages.microsoft.com/config/debian/12
curl $URL/packages-microsoft-prod.deb \
    -o packages-microsoft-prod.deb
dpkg -i packages-microsoft-prod.deb
apt-get update && apt-get install -y dotnet-sdk-6.0
su jenkins
dotnet tool install --global Pickles.CommandLine
```

</> Example #40: Running Pickles through a Jenkins pipeline

Let's extend the previous example and generate documentation when your Jenkins build runs, and also use some additional features of Pickles.

 Groovy

First, add a **json** formatter writing to `./build/reports/results.json` to your Cucumber CI profiles. Then update `./vars/buildPipeline.groovy`:

```groovy
stage('Test') {
    try {
        tests.executeCucumberTests([
            language: language
        ])
    } finally {
        def appName = 'simple search page'
        def fdir = language == 'java' ? './src/test/resources' : './features'
        sh """
        APP_VERSION=`git rev-parse --short=8 HEAD`
        ~/.dotnet/tools/pickles \
            -f $fdir -o ./build/docs --df=word \
            -l en --sn="$appName" --sv="\$APP_VERSION" \
            --trfmt=cucumberjson --lr=./build/reports/results.json
        """
        archiveArtifacts artifacts: 'build/**/*', fingerprint: true
        junit 'build/reports/**/*.xml'
    }
}
```

Pickles will generate a report containing your features and their test status. This document will also be archived to the Jenkins build.

Chapter 10: Building a Test Framework

Between step design and planning, building out step definitions and scenarios, improving the performing of your test suites, and executing those test suites in a CI/CD pipeline, what started out as a few simple step definitions has expanded into an entire test framework. In this chapter, we'll look at some additional functionality to consider adding to your step definitions to take your test automation to the next level.

10.1 Defining a Test Configuration

As your test suite becomes more sophisticated, there will be common configuration values that you will want to be able to set for different environments or different parts of your CI/CD pipeline. Some implementations of Cucumber provide a built-in mechanism for managing configuration while others do not. We will take a look at how to utilize that functionality as well as some alternative approaches.

10.1.1 Using Environment Variables

If your test suite needs a few simple configuration options, you can use environment variables in the terminal. Accessing environment variables is also very straightforward:

- Java: `System.getEnv("VALUE")`
- JavaScript (NodeJS): `process.env.VALUE`
- Ruby: `ENV['VALUE']`

You can set environment variables in the terminal using `export VAR=VALUE` if you're using `bash` and most other shells, or `set VAR=VALUE` for `cmd`.

10.1.2 Using Cucumber Profiles

 **Ruby**

You can define profiles in the `./cucumber.yml` file in your project:

```
default: VALUE='123' --tags "not @wip"
wip: VALUE='123' --tags @wip
```

To use profiles, open a terminal and run `cucumber --profile <name>`

You can also pass parameters directly, for example:

```
cucumber VALUE='123' --tags @wip
```

⊟ Java

This functionality is not supported by CucumberJVM;[85] however, you can use `System.getProperty(String)`[86] and then pass parameters using the -D command-line flag:

```
java -DVALUE='123' ...
```

You can also use Maven profiles to set up different build targets with various CucumberJVM parameters. Add the following to the end of your `pom.xml`:

```xml
<project xmlns="http://maven.apache.org/POM/4.0.0"
    xmlns:xsi="http://www.w3.org/2001/XMLSchema-instance"
    xsi:schemaLocation="http://maven.apache.org/POM/4.0.0
    http://maven.apache.org/xsd/maven-4.0.0.xsd">
  <build>
    <!-- Build Configuration... -->
  </build>
  <profiles>
    <profile>
      <id>smoke-tests</id>
      <build>
        <plugins>
          <plugin>
            <groupId>org.apache.maven.plugins</groupId>
            <artifactId>maven-surefire-plugin</artifactId>
            <configuration>
              <properties>
                <configurationParameters>
                  cucumber.filter.tags=@smoke
                  cucumber.publish.quiet=true
                </configurationParameters>
              </properties>
            </configuration>
          </plugin>
        </plugins>
      </build>
    </profile>
  </profiles>
</project>
```

You can target this profile when running Maven: `mvn test -Psmoke-tests`

⚠ **Pitfall:** The Cucumber Java Skeleton project has a file called `RunCucumberTest.java` that sets the `cucumber.plugin` parameter. You will need to remove the `@ConfigurationParameter` annotation with key `PLUGIN_PROPERTY_NAME` in order to be able to set it through Maven. This parameter allows you to set one or more formatters, so you will want to be able to customize this parameter for different types of builds.

---

[85] https://cucumber.io/docs/cucumber/configuration/?lang=java#profiles
[86] https://www.tutorialspoint.com/system-getproperty-in-java

📜 JavaScript

You can define profiles in the `./cucumber.js` file[87] in your project:

```javascript
module.exports = {
    'default': {
        tags: 'not @wip',
        worldParameters: { VALUE: '...' }
    },
    'wip': {
        tags: '@wip',
        worldParameters: { VALUE: '...' }
    }
};
```

To use profiles, open a terminal and run `cucumber.js --profile <name>`

You can also pass parameters directly, for example:

```
cucumber.js --world-parameters '{"VALUE":"..."}' --tags @wip
```

10.1.3 Using Third-Party Configuration Libraries

For more complex configuration requirements, it is recommended to use a configuration file in conjunction with a library that can manage loading the appropriate environment.

🏅 **Pro Tip:** Use YAML for configuration files since it is more flexible and easier to read than JSON.

If you anticipate a test suite to scale beyond a small and simple set of scenarios, setting up a robust configuration system with support for multiple environments will simplify integrating your test suite with a CI/CD pipeline.

</> Example #41: Integrating a Configuration Library

💎 Ruby

You can use a gem package such as ruby-config to manage multiple configurations. Run `gem install config` to get started,[88] then create a `./config` directory for the YAML configuration files. For example:

```ruby
require 'config'

Config.load_and_set_settings(
    Config.setting_files('config', ENV['TEST_ENV'] || 'default')
)

Given('a test value is printed') do
    puts Settings.steps.testValue
end
```

---

[87] https://github.com/cucumber/cucumber-js/blob/main/docs/profiles.md
[88] https://github.com/rubyconfig/config?tab=readme-ov-file#installing

☕ Java

You can use a library such as java-config to manage multiple configurations.
Add `com.typesafe.config` to your `./pom.xml` to get started,[89] then create
configuration files in your `resources` directory. Configuration files can be
in JSON or HOCON. You will also need to call `ConfigFactory.load` to
load your configuration data, which also allows you to set the environment.
It is recommended you use an environment variable and pass the value using
`System.getEnv`. Here is an example of integrating your configuration with
a step definition:

```java
import com.typesafe.config.*;
import io.cucumber.java.en.Given;

public class MySteps {

    @Given("a test value is printed")
    public void given_a_test_value_is_printed() {
        Config config = ConfigFactory.load(System.getEnv("TEST_ENV"));
        System.out.println(config.getString("steps.testValue"));
    }
}
```

📜 JavaScript

You can use an NPM package such as node-config to manage multiple
configurations. Run `npm install config js-yaml` to get started,[90] then
create a `./config` directory in your project. Your configuration files can be
one of many formats, including JSON or YAML. You can set the environment
using the `NODE_ENV` environment variable. Here is an example of integrating
your configuration with a step definition:

```javascript
const { Given } = require('@cucumber/cucumber');
const config = require('config');

Given('a test value is printed', function() {
    console.log(config.steps.testValue);
});
```

⚠️ **Pitfall:** If you're using Git for source control (you *are* using source
control, right?), add these lines to your `.gitignore` file to avoid accidentally
committing sensitive information to your repository:

```
config/*
!config/default.*
```

🏅 **Pro Tip:** Add your test configuration to the scenario context or `World`
object so that your configuration is easily accessible to your step definitions.

---

[89] https://github.com/lightbend/config
[90] https://www.npmjs.com/package/config

10.2 Managing Logs

As your tests become more complex, debugging them when they behave
unexpectedly becomes more difficult. Without good logging, it can be
difficult to determine whether your application or your tests are the source
of the failure, causing confusion that negatively affects your team's confidence
in the reliability of the automated tests. While step definitions can write
messages to stdout[91] without any additional libraries, this simple form of
logging may not be sufficient as your tests grow.

10.2.1 Log Levels

One advantage to using a logging library over writing messages to stdout
directly is that you can categorize your log messages into levels. Common
log levels include *error*, *warning*, *info*, and *debug*. Once you have your levels
configured, you can decide which ones need to be displayed depending on
how you are running your tests. For instance, you probably don't want
debugging messages during a typical CI/CD build, but you'll want to be
able to turn on debugging if you're researching a failing test locally.

When you configure the log level for your application, you will get output
for that log level as well as any other log levels that are of a higher criticality.
For example, if your application's log level is set to *info* you will get *info*,
warning, and *error* messages.

10.2.2 Log Formats

When creating log messages in your application, there is additional metadata
associated with those individual messages such as the timestamp when
the message occurred, the current user, etc. There are different ways of
storing and displaying this information, so logging libraries support different
formatters, which allows you to control the way the log messages are rendered
to a log sink.

If you want to store the logs for later analysis, you may want to output
them in a format like JSON, which preserves the integrity of the underlying
data. Alternatively, if you want a person to be able to quickly and easily
read the logs, a "pretty" formatter would be more appropriate.

10.2.3 Log Sinks

Another advantage of using a logging library is the ability to configure one
or more log sinks, also known as "appenders" or "transports" depending on
which library you're using. These allow you to direct the output of your
logs to one or more destinations such as a file, database, or external server.

---

[91] https://www.linfo.org/standard_output.html

10.2.4 Log Instances

One more reason to use a logging library instead of writing to stdout is the fact that you can create multiple loggers in your application. For example, if part of your test suite interacts with HTTP-based APIs while another interacts with a web browser UI using Selenium WebDriver, you would want the ability to log those entries separately.

</> Example #42: Integrating a Logging Library

◇ Ruby

You can use a logging library such as `logging` to manage your logs. Run `gem install logging` to get started.[92]

```ruby
require 'logging'

log = Logging.logger['example_logger']
log.level = :info

log.add_appenders \
    Logging.appenders.stdout(level: :warn),
    Logging.appenders.file('output.log', layout: Logging.layouts.json)

Given('test values are logged') do
    log.debug 'this message will not be seen because of the log level.'
    log.info 'this message will be in the file but not shown on the screen.'
    log.warn 'this message will be in both the file and on the screen.'
end
```

🏅 Pro Tip: If you have more than one step definition file, initialize your loggers in `./features/support/env.rb` so they can be shared across all of your step definition files:

```ruby
require 'logging'

$log = Logging.logger['example_logger']
$log.level = :info

$log.add_appenders \
    Logging.appenders.stdout(level: :warn),
    Logging.appenders.file('output.log', layout: Logging.layouts.json)
```

In your step definitions file:

```ruby
Given('test values are logged') do
    $log.warn 'this message will be in both the file and on the screen.'
end
```

---

[92] https://github.com/TwP/logging

🖥 Java

You can use a logging library such as Log4J to manage your logs.[93] To get started, update your `./pom.xml` file:

```xml
<dependency>
    <groupId>org.apache.logging.log4j</groupId><artifactId>log4j-api</artifactId>
    <version>2.23.1</version>
</dependency>
<dependency>
    <groupId>org.apache.logging.log4j</groupId><artifactId>log4j-core</artifactId>
    <version>2.23.1</version>
</dependency>
```

⚠ **Caution:** Be advised of CVE-2021-44228,[94] also referred to as "Log4Shell." If you are using Log4J, use version 2.20.0 or higher.

First, create a `log4j.properties` file:

```properties
log4j.rootLogger=INFO, file, stdout
log4j.appender.file=org.apache.log4j.FileAppender
log4j.appender.file.File=output.log
log4j.appender.file.layout=org.apache.log4j.JsonTemplateLayout
log4j.appender.stdout=org.apache.log4j.ConsoleAppender
log4j.appender.stdout.Target=System.out
log4j.appender.stdout.layout=org.apache.log4j.PatternLayout
log4j.appender.stdout.layout.ConversionPattern=%-5p [%t]: %m%n
```

You can then add logging to your step definition file:

```java
import io.cucumber.java.en.Given;
import org.apache.logging.log4j.Logger;

public class MySteps {
    private static final Logger log = LogManager.getLogger(MySteps.class);

    @Given("test values are logged")
    public void given_test_values_are_logged() {
        log.debug("this message will not be seen because of the log level.");
        log.info("this message will be in the file but not shown on the screen.");
        log.warn("this message will be in both the file and on the screen.");
    }
}
```

For more information on configuring Log4J, review the documentation.[95]

---

[93] https://logging.apache.org/log4j/2.x/maven-artifacts.html
[94] https://nvd.nist.gov/vuln/detail/CVE-2021-44228
[95] https://logging.apache.org/log4j/2.x/manual/configuration.html

📜 **JavaScript**

You can use a logging library such as Winston to manage your logs. Run `npm install winston` to get started.[96]

```javascript
const { Given } = require('@cucumber/cucumber');
const { createLogger, format, transports } = require('winston');

const log = createLogger({
    level: 'info',
    format: format.simple(),
    transports: [
        new transports.Console({ level: 'warn' }),
        new transports.File({
            filename: 'output.log',
            format: format.combine(format.timestamp(), format.json())
        })
    ]
});

Given('test values are logged', function() {
    log.debug('this message will not be seen because of the log level.');
    log.info('this message will be in the file but not shown on the screen.');
    log.warn('this message will be in both the file and on the screen.');
});
```

⚠️ **Caution:** If you have more than one step definition file, initialize your loggers in one place.

⚠️ **Pitfall:** By default, Winston does not include a timestamp even when formatting the output as JSON. You will have to use `winston.format.combine()` as demonstrated above to add the timestamp.

🏅 **Pro Tip:** Consider storing your logging configuration in the test configuration file that you implemented in the previous section so that your logging configuration can automatically adjust based on the environment you are running your tests in.

---

[96] https://www.npmjs.com/package/winston

10.3 Loading Test Data

When performing testing of a larger application, you may need test data
to generate user accounts, orders, etc. You can use existing libraries to
generate data or load your own custom data as part of your testing.

10.3.1 Using Faker

</> Example #43: Generating Fake User Data

You can generate user data by using any language-specific version of Faker,
all of which are ports of the original library written in Perl.

Ruby

Faker[97] is a popular library for generating fake account information in Ruby.
To get started, run `gem install faker`.

```ruby
require 'faker'

def generate_user_account
    name = Faker::Name.name
    city = Faker::Address.city
    state = Faker::Address.state
    phone_number = Faker::PhoneNumber.phone_number
    email_local = name.downcase.gsub(/\s+/, '.').gsub(/[^a-z0-9.]/, '')
    email_address = "#{email_local}@sink.mywebsite.com"

    {
        name: name,
        email: email_address,
        city: city,
        state: state,
        phone_number: phone_number
    }
end
```

Pro Tip: When performing end-to-end testing with email addresses,
make sure that emails are sent to a "sink account" to avoid sending messages
to real accounts.

Java

Faker[98] can generate fake account information in Java. To get started,
update your `./pom.xml`:

```xml
<dependency>
    <groupId>com.github.javafaker</groupId><artifactId>javafaker</artifactId>
    <version>1.0.2</version><scope>test</scope>
</dependency>
```

---

[97] https://rubygems.org/gems/faker/
[98] https://github.com/DiUS/java-faker

Assuming your application has a **UserAccount** class, generate accounts:

```java
import com.github.javafaker.Faker;
import java.util.regex.Matcher;
import java.util.regex.Pattern;

public class UserAccountGenerator {

    public static UserAccount generateUserAccount() {
        Faker faker = new Faker();
        String name = faker.name().fullName();
        String city = faker.address().city();
        String state = faker.address().state();
        String phone = faker.phoneNumber().phoneNumber();

        String emailLocalPart = name.toLowerCase().replace(" ", ".");
        emailLocalPart = emailLocalPart.replaceAll("[^a-z0-9.]", "");
        String email = emailLocalPart + "@sink.mywebsite.com";

        return new UserAccount(name, email, city, state, phone);
    }
}
```

JavaScript

You can use the Faker[99] library to generate fake account data in JavaScript.
To get started, run **npm install @faker-js/faker --save-dev**.

```javascript
const { faker } = require('@faker-js/faker');

function generateUserAccount() {
    const name = faker.name.findName();
    const city = faker.address.city();
    const state = faker.address.state();
    const phoneNumber = faker.phone.phoneNumber();

    const emailLocalPart = name.toLowerCase()
        .replace(/\s+/g, '.')
        .replace(/[^a-z0-9.]/g, '');
    const email = `${emailLocalPart}@sink.mywebsite.com`;

    return { name, email, city, state, phoneNumber };
}

module.exports = { generateUserAccount };
```

🛑 **Danger:** The original NPM package **faker** was intentionally broken by its author in protest of for-profit companies utilizing open-source software without giving back to the community. Soon after, this same author added an infinite loop into **colors**, resulting in the NPM colors attack.[100]

10.3.2 Loading External Resources

Let's take a look at how to easily load test data from files into Cucumber by using a resource manager. You can extend this example to parse different types of files as needed.

---

[99]https://fakerjs.dev/
[100]https://news.ycombinator.com/item?id=29877745

</> **Example #44:** Loading Files into Cucumber

◇ Ruby

Create a file `./features/utils/resources.rb`:

```ruby
$resources ||= {}
def load_resource(name)
    return $resources[name] if $resources.key?(name)

    file_path = Dir.glob("./resources/#{name}.*").first
    return nil unless file_path

    extension = File.extname(file_path)
    content = if extension.downcase == '.txt'
                  File.read(file_path)
              else
                  File.binread(file_path).bytes
              end
    $resources[name] = content
end
```

In your step definitions:

```ruby
Given('some file is loaded') { @data = load_resource 'someFile' }
```

▤ Java

Create a file `./src/test/java/<Pkg Path>/ResourceManager.java`:

```java
public class ResourceManager {
    private final Map<String, Object> cache = new HashMap<>();
    public Object loadResource(String name) {
        if (cache.containsKey(name)) { return cache.get(name); }
        File folder = new File("./src/test/resources");
        File[] files = folder.listFiles((dir, f) -> f.startsWith(name + "."));
        if (files == null || files.length == 0) { return null; }
        String extension = files[0].getName().substring(
            files[0].getName().lastIndexOf('.') + 1);
        Object content = null;
        try {
            if (extension == "txt") {
                content = Files.readString(files[0].toPath());
            } else { content = Files.readAllBytes(files[0].toPath()); }
        } catch (Exception e) { return null; }
        cache.put(name, content);
        return content;
    }
}
```

To use `ResourceManager`, add it to `CustomWorld`:

```java
public class CustomWorld {
    private ResourceManager resources = new ResourceManager();
    // ...existing code...
    public ResourceManager getResources() { return resources; }
}
```

Now you can access it from your step definitions:

```java
public class MySteps {
    private CustomWorld world;
    public MySteps(CustomWorld world) {
        this.world = world;
    }

    @Given
    public void given_some_file_is_loaded() {
        String data = (String)world.getResources().loadResource("someFile");
    }
}
```

JavaScript

Create a file `./features/utils/resources.js`:

```javascript
const fs = require('fs');
const path = require('path');
const cache = {};

function loadResource(name) {
    if (cache[name]) { return cache[name]; }
    const resourcesDir = path.join(process.cwd(), 'resources');
    const files = fs.readdirSync(resourcesDir);
    const file = files.find(f => path.basename(f, path.extname(f)) === name);
    if (!file) { return null; }
    const fullPath = path.join(resourcesDir, file);
    const extension = path.extname(file).toLowerCase();
    let content;
    switch (extension) {
    case '.txt':
        content = fs.readFileSync(fullPath, 'utf8');
        break;
    default:
        content = fs.readFileSync(fullPath);
        break;
    }
    cache[name] = content;
    return content;
}

const resources = new Proxy({}, {
    get: function(t, p, r) { return loadResource(p); }
});

module.exports = { loadResource, resources };
```

In your step definition:

```javascript
const { Before, Given } = require('@cucumber/cucumber');
const { resources } = require('../utils/resources');

Before(function () { this.resources = resources; });

Given('some file is loaded', function () {
    const data = this.resources.someFile;
});
```

Pro Tip: Add additional file extension handlers to parse different file formats such as JSON and YAML.

10.4 Debugging Cucumber

As your step definition code grows, understanding the behavior of your
tests becomes more complicated. Debugging tools can help you to better
understand the behavior of your tests and locate bugs faster.

10.4.1 Debugging with IntelliJ

If you are using RubyMine, IntelliJ IDEA, or WebStorm and you have
installed the required Cucumber plugins mentioned in **Chapter 3**, the
built-in debugger should be ready to use without additional configuration.

10.4.2 Debugging with Visual Studio Code

Debugging Cucumber in Visual Studio Code requires a little more configuration depending on which language you are using.

 **Ruby**

Install the Ruby LSP[101] and VSCode rdbg Ruby Debugger[102] extensions
for Visual Studio Code. Also run `gem install debug rdbg`. Then create
a file `./.vscode/launch.json`:

```json
{
    "version": "0.2.0",
    "configurations": [{
        "type": "rdbg",
        "name": "Cucumber",
        "request": "launch",
        "script": "features/**/*.feature",
        "command": "cucumber"
    }]
}
```

Now you can start debugging by pressing **F5**. If you have set any breakpoints
in your `.rb` files, the debugger will let you step through the code.

⚠ **Pitfall:** Most examples of debugging Ruby with VS Code reference
the Ruby[103] extension; however, this extension has been deprecated.

---

[101] https://marketplace.visualstudio.com/items?itemName=Shopify.ruby-lsp
[102] https://marketplace.visualstudio.com/items?itemName=KoichiSasada.vscode-rdbg
[103] https://marketplace.visualstudio.com/items?itemName=rebornix.Ruby

📇 Java

Install the Extension Pack for Java[104] extension for Visual Studio Code. To debug your tests, navigate to the "Testing" Activity Bar on the left side of the screen (the icon is a beaker). Expand the tree and click the "Debug Test" button (the icon is a play button with a bug on it) next to `RunCucumberTest`. If you have set any breakpoints in your `.java` files, the debugger will let you step through the code.

📜 JavaScript

While there are several ways to configure NodeJS debugging, I would recommend using the "auto attach" method. Open the Command Palette with keyboard shortcut `Ctrl + Shift + P` and run the "Debug: Toggle Auto Attach" command. Set the auto attach setting to the "only with flag" option, then restart the application.

In your `./package.json` file, add a new script command:

```
{
    "scripts": {
        "test:debug": "node --inspect ./node_modules/.bin/cucumber-js"
    }
}
```

Now when you run `npm run test:debug` in the terminal, Visual Studio Code will auto-attach the debugger for you and pause if any breakpoints are hit.

10.4.3 Debugging with Logs

In **10.2 Managing Logs** we discussed how to add advanced logging to your Cucumber tests. As powerful as debuggers are, sometimes collecting data in CI/CD at the time of a test failure will provide more valuable information, especially if the scenarios in question are not consistently failing. Re-creating a failure on your local machine may be difficult or impossible because of changing network conditions, differences between your local machine and the server/cloud, or timing problems caused by unlikely combinations of events.

🏅 **Pro Tip:** If you are performing UI testing, capture a screenshot of your application's UI whenever a scenario fails with an `After` hook, and archive the screenshot to the build in Jenkins. Being able to look at the UI at the time of a failure can often reveal the root cause of a test failure. After all, a picture is worth a thousand words!

---

[104] https://marketplace.visualstudio.com/items?itemName=vscjava.vscode-java-pack

10.5 Advanced Parameter Processing

All the versions of Cucumber we've looked at so far support custom parameter types; however, there are cases where you may want to have control over all parameter processing. Since all values coming from Gherkin start off as strings, having the ability to manage the transformation of parameter values as they come through Cucumber allows for more fine-grained control over how the data from Gherkin behaves in your step definitions.

</> Example #45: Building a Parameter Transformer

◇ Ruby

While Cucumber in Ruby does not have a built-in way of transforming parameters other than custom parameter types, you can implement your own transformer for your step definitions and add it to your step library.

```ruby
def transformer(&stepdef)
    proc { |*args|
        # do something with the args...
        instance_exec(*args, &stepdef)
    }
end

Given('the user adds {int} items', transformer do |i|
    # transformed args will be passed here.
end)
```

⚠ Caution: You will have to make sure that all step definitions within your step library make use of this **transformer** function or the code will not run since Cucumber itself isn't managing the execution of this function.

⊟ Java

In CucumberJVM, you can specify default transformers for parameters and data tables. You can combine these bindings with an object mapper to change the way data is converted.

⚠ Pitfall: CucumberJVM will only call the default transformer functions if parameters or data table values need to be converted to an unknown type.

```java
import com.fasterxml.jackson.databind.ObjectMapper;

public class TransformerHooks {
    private final ObjectMapper mapper = new ObjectMapper();

    @DefaultParameterTransformer
    @DefaultDataTableCellTransformer
    public Object transformer(Object value, Type type) {
        return mapper.convertValue(value, mapper.constructType(type));
    }
}
```

You can also implement your own **transformer** method to wrap step definitions in CucumberJVM in a similar approach to the examples provided in Ruby and JavaScript. First, create a **TransformableSteps.java** file:

```java
import java.util.function.BiConsumer;

public abstract class TransformableSteps {
    protected <T, U> BiConsumer<T, U> transformer(BiConsumer<T, U> step) {
        return (arg1, arg2) -> { /* transform here */ step.accept(arg1, arg2); };
    }
}
```

Then extend your step class with **TransformableSteps**:

```java
public class Steps extends TransformableSteps {
    @Given("the user adds {int} items")
    public void the_user_adds_n_items(int items) {
        transformer((Integer _items, Integer extra1) -> {
            // your step definition code goes here.
        }).accept(items, null);
    }
}
```

JavaScript

You can create advanced custom integrations with CucumberJS using the **setDefinitionFunctionWrapper** API. The example below demonstrates an implementation of a wrapper function for promises and callbacks.

```javascript
const { setDefinitionFunctionWrapper } = require('@cucumber/cucumber');

function doTransform(args) { /* do something with the args. */ return args; }

setDefinitionFunctionWrapper(fn => async function step(...args) {
    const result = await fn.apply(this, doTransform.call(this, args));
    return result;
});
```

Alternatively, you could use a **transformer** function on a per-step basis similarly to how we implemented it in Ruby and Java.

```javascript
const { Given } = require('@cucumber/cucumber');

function doTransform(args) {
    // do something with the args.
    return args;
}

function transformer(fn) {
    return async function step(...args) {
        const result = await fn.apply(this, doTransform.call(this, args));
        return result;
    };
}

Given('the user adds {int} items', transformer(async function (i) {
    // transformed args will be passed here.
}));
```

10.6 Integrating a Template Engine

This is probably the most controversial section in this book. Many would argue that introducing the ability to use placeholders within your feature file parameters and tables introduces too much of a "programming-like" experience to Gherkin, and contradicts the goal of keeping tests as human-readable as possible. There is a trade-off to be made: if you choose to use templates, you will be able to build a smaller set of more powerful step definitions, but those step definitions will be more complex.

10.6.1 What Is a Template Engine?

A template engine is a software library that takes a model object and a template string as inputs, and then produces an output string by replacing placeholders in the template string with values from the model object:

Template	Model	Output
`Hello, {{name}}!`	`{ "name": "world" }`	`Hello, world!`

Handlebars: A minimalist template engine with many advanced features and extensibility. I have used this engine for many projects and find it to be very powerful because it offers many features and customizations without allowing "code" to appear in the templates. It is also supported across multiple languages:

- Ruby: `ruby-handlebars`[105]
- Java: `handlebars.java`[106]
- JavaScript: `handlebars.js`[107]

🏅 **Pro Tip:** Handlebars was originally designed as an HTML template engine, so by default it HTML-encodes all output unless you use the "triple stash" syntax. You can turn this off in JavaScript when compiling: `Handlebars.compile(template, { noEscape: true });`[108]

ES6 Templates: This format is used in JavaScript and NodeJS and can be utilized with the `es6-dynamic-template` NPM package.[109] There is not a Ruby or Java library that supports this specific template format.

⚠️ **Pitfall:** While it is possible to use engines such as lo-dash templates, EJS, ERB, Groovy, or even (shudder) `eval()`, we don't want to have code appear in our feature files, and since these engines encourage that approach, they are not recommended for integrating with Cucumber.

---

[105] https://github.com/SmartBear/ruby-handlebars
[106] https://github.com/jknack/handlebars.java
[107] https://github.com/handlebars-lang/handlebars.js
[108] https://stackoverflow.com/a/9860629/1267688
[109] https://www.npmjs.com/package/es6-dynamic-template

10.6.2 Handlebars and Cucumber

</> **Example #46:** Using Handlebars with Cucumber

```
Feature: Demonstrate a Handlebars Template with Cucumber

Scenario: Using a Handlebars Parameter
    Given the user "{{users.Jim}}" logs in
```

All the following Handlebars examples will use the `transformer` code that
we implemented in **10.5**. We will also be passing a world object as the model
for all calls to Handlebars. Passing the scenario context to Handlebars gives
your templates access to all the data relevant to your running scenario.

◈ Ruby

```ruby
require 'ruby-handlebars'

$hbs = Handlebars::Handlebars.new

module CustomWorld
    attr_accessor :users
end

World(world: CustomWorld)

def transformer(&stepdef)
    proc { |*args|
        result = args.map do |arg|
            if arg.is_a?(String)
                $hbs.compile(arg).call(world)
            else
                arg
            end
        end
        instance_exec(*result, &stepdef)
    }
end

Given('the user {string} logs in', transformer do |user|
    # do something with the user.
end)
```

In this example, the `CustomWorld` module is assigned to `world` so that it
can be referenced both in the step definitions and passed as the model value
for Handlebars.

▣ Java

For CucumberJVM, we will be combining the example from **10.5** as well as
utilizing dependency injection for loading the world object from **6.4.2**.

🏅 **Pro Tip:** Consider adding `try/catch` or `rescue` blocks around code
that executes templates so that if something fails, your code can fall back
gracefully and return the original value while writing failure messages to
your logging instead.

Add additional code to your **TransformableSteps** class:

```java
import com.github.jknack.handlebars.*;

public abstract class TransformableSteps {
    protected CustomWorld world;
    private final Handlebars hbs = new Handlebars();

    public TransformableSteps(CustomWorld world) {
        this.world = world;
    }

    protected Object transformValue(Object value) {
        try {
            if (value instanceof String) {
                Template t = hbs.compile((String)value);
                return t.apply(world);
            }
        } catch (Exception ex) { return value; }
    }

    protected <T, U> BiConsumer<T, U> transformer(BiConsumer<T, U> step) {
        return (arg1, arg2) -> {
            step.accept(transformValue(arg1), transformValue(arg2));
        };
    }
}
```

In your step definitions class:

```java
public class Steps extends TransformableSteps {
    public Steps(CustomWorld world) {
        super(world);
    }

    @Given("the user adds {int} items")
    public void the_user_adds_n_items(int items) {
        transformer((Integer _items, Integer extra1) -> {
            // your step definition code goes here.
        }).accept(items, null);
    }
}
```

JavaScript

In this example, it is assumed that a wrapper is registered using
setDefinitionFunctionWrapper to automatically transform all step
parameters from **10.5**.

```javascript
const Handlebars = require('handlebars');

function doTransform(args) {
    const result = args.map((arg) => {
        if (typeof arg === 'string' || arg instanceof String) {
            arg = Handlebars.compile(arg).call(null, this);
        }
        return arg;
    });
    return result;
}
```

10.6.3 Handlebars and Data Table Parameters

Processing data table values through Ruby and JavaScript requires extending the previous example to look for a step definition argument type `DataTable`. From there, we can use `map` to iterate and reconstruct the table after applying our template function to provide the processed table data to the downstream step definition code. We are also going to refactor the transform to implement custom hooks so we can extend our code later.

🏅 **Pro Tip:** Consider caching template functions by using a hash table to look up templates you've already compiled. If a template runs more than once during a test run, caching can improve performance.

</> **Example #47:** Processing Data Table Parameters with Handlebars

◇ **Ruby**

Write your transformer code to `./features/support/transformer.rb`:

```ruby
$param_transform_callbacks = []
$dt_cell_transform_callbacks = []

module CustomWorld
    attr_accessor :item, :user1
end
World(context: CustomWorld)

def parameter_transformer(&callback)
    $param_transform_callbacks.append(callback)
end

def data_table_cell_transformer(&callback)
    $dt_cell_transform_callbacks.append(callback)
end

def transformer(&stepdef)
    process_val = proc do |val, callbacks|
        if val.is_a?(Cucumber::MultilineArgument::DataTable)
            tbl = Cucumber::Core::Test::DataTable.new(val.hashes.map do |row|
                row.transform_values do |v|
                    instance_exec(v, $dt_cell_transform_callbacks, &process_val)
                end
            end)
            Cucumber::MultilineArgument::DataTable.new(tbl)
        else
            result = val
            callbacks.each do |cb|
                result = instance_exec(result, &cb)
            end
            result
        end
    end
    proc { |*args|
        result = args.map do |arg|
            instance_exec(arg, $param_transform_callbacks, &process_val)
        end
        instance_exec(*result, &stepdef)
    }
end
```

Besides processing data table values individually, you could also create a
`data_table_entry_transformer`. The hook would need to have a way of
resolving the table row into a Ruby class type and then construct an object
of that type.

In a file `./features/support/hbs.rb`:

```ruby
$hbs = Handlebars::Handlebars.new
$templates = {}

parameter_transformer do |val|
    if val.is_a?(String)
        $templates[val] ||= $hbs.compile(val)
        $templates[val].call(context)
    else
        val
    end
rescue StandardError => e
    val
end

data_table_cell_transformer do |val|
    if val.is_a?(String)
        $templates[val] ||= $hbs.compile(val)
        $templates[val].call(context)
    else
        val
    end
rescue StandardError => e
    val
end
```

⚠️ **Pitfall:** While catching and ignoring template processing errors is
recommended, consider writing any exceptions as warning messages to the
logging you configured in **10.2 Managing Logs**. Silently losing the errors
could result in unexpected behaviors that negatively affect the reliability of
your tests.

🏅 **Pro Tip:** Add Handlebars helper functions to handle time calculations,
formatting, and other common functionality you may need to implement in
your Gherkin feature files. We'll look at some examples of helper functions
in the next section.

▣ Java

You can continue to extend the `TransformableSteps` to add support for Handlebars within data table parameters in CucumberJVM. Let's also implement template caching to improve performance.

```java
import com.github.jknack.handlebars.*;
import io.cucumber.java.DataTable;

import java.util.HashMap;
import java.util.List;
import java.util.Map;

public abstract class TransformableSteps {
    private final Map<String, Template> templates = new HashMap<String, Template>();

    protected String transformString(String value) {
        try {
            Template t = templates.putIfAbsent((String)value,
                handlebars.compile((String)value));
            return t.apply(world);
        } catch (Exception ex) { return value; }
    }

    protected DataTable transformDataTable(DataTable table) {
        try {
            List<List<String>> originalRows = table.asLists(String.class);
            List<List<String>> transformedRows = originalRows.stream()
                    .map(row -> row.stream()
                            .map(this::transformValue)
                            .collect(Collectors.toList())))
                    .collect(Collectors.toList());

            return DataTable.create(transformedRows);
        } catch (Exception ex) { return table; }
    }

    protected Object transformValue(Object value) {
        if (value instanceof String) {
            return transformString((String)value);
        } else if (value instanceof DataTable) {
            return transformDataTable((DataTable)value);
        }
        return value;
    }
    // ...existing code...
}
```

🏅 **Pro Tip:** You can overload the `transformer` method to avoid the "extra parameter" problem we saw in the previous example. For an example of this, look at the source code for the Java 8 version of CucumberJVM and you will see method overloads for the lambda versions of `Given`, `When`, and `Then`, which can accept lambda step definitions with between zero and nine arguments.[110]

---

[110] https://javadoc.io/doc/io.cucumber/cucumber-java8/latest/io/cucumber/java8/En.html

📜 JavaScript

Similarly to the Ruby implementation, our `transformer` function can look for a step definition argument containing a data table and process it accordingly. We can also refactor the code here as well.

```javascript
const { setDefinitionFunctionWrapper, DataTable } = require('@cucumber/cucumber');

let param_transform_callbacks = [];
let dt_cell_transform_callbacks = [];

function ParameterTransformer(callback) {
    param_transform_callbacks.push(callback);
}

function DataTableCellTransformer(callback) {
    dt_cell_transform_callbacks.push(callback);
}

function doTransform(args) {
    const processVal = (val, callbacks) => {
        if (val && val.raw && typeof val.raw === 'function') {
            return new DataTable(val.raw().map(row => row.map((v) => {
                return processVal(v, dt_cell_transform_callbacks);
            })));
        }
        let result = val;
        callbacks.forEach((cb) => {
            result = cb.call(this, result);
        });
        return result;
    };
    return args.map(arg => processVal(arg, param_transform_callbacks));
}

setDefinitionFunctionWrapper(fn => async function step(...args) {
    const result = await fn.apply(this, doTransform.call(this, args));
    return result;
});

module.exports = { ParameterTransformer, DataTableCellTransformer };
```

You can now register your custom hooks as shown below:

```javascript
const Handlebars = require('handlebars');
const { ParameterTransformer, DataTableCellTransformer } = require('./transformer');
let templates = {};

function processTemplate(context, val) {
    if (typeof val === 'string' || val instanceof String) {
        templates[val] = templates[val] || Handlebars.compile(val);
        return templates[val].call(null, context);
    }
    return val;
}

function hook(val) {
    try { return processTemplate(this, val); }
    catch (err) { return val; }
}

ParameterTransformer(hook);
DataTableCellTransformer(hook);
```

10.6.4 Using Handlebars Helpers

Another feature of Handlebars that makes it a very powerful tool for testing is its ability to support helper functions. You can build both inline helper functions and whole block helpers.

</> Example #48: Using an Inline Helper

Let's write an inline helper that can read data from the test configuration. In this way, you can inject environment-specific data into your feature files directly. This helper will be called `config` and can be used as shown here: `{{config 'http.baseUrl'}}`.

Ruby

In your `./features/support/hbs.rb` file, add your helper registrations.

```ruby
# ...assuming that you've already loaded your configuration...

$hbs.register_helper('config') do |context, value|
    value.to_s.split('.').reduce(Settings) do |acc, method|
        acc.send(method)
    end
end
```

Java

Registering helpers with Handlebars in Java is a similar process, so let's add some code to the constructor for `TransformableSteps`:

```java
import com.github.jknack.handlebars.*;
import com.typesafe.config.*;

public abstract class TransformableSteps {
    // ...existing code...
    protected Config config;

    public TransformableSteps(CustomWorld world) {
        // ...existing code...
        String env = System.getenv("TEST_ENV");
        this.config = ConfigFactory.load(env != null ? env : "default");
        handlebars.registerHelper("config", new Helper<String>() {
            public CharSequence apply(String value, Options options) {
                return new Handlebars.SafeString(config.getString(value));
            }
        });
    } // ..existing code...
}
```

JavaScript

Registering helpers in JavaScript is similar to the other languages.

```javascript
const Handlebars = require('handlebars');
const config = require('config');

Handlebars.registerHelper('config', (v) => config.get(v));
```

10.7 Using TypeScript with CucumberJS

Many software development teams are switching from "vanilla" JavaScript to TypeScript in order to write code with fewer runtime errors and to make use of modern frameworks that use elements of the TypeScript syntax. CucumberJS itself was converted to TypeScript in version 7, so all the type definitions already exist, which allows you to write your own step definitions in TypeScript.

10.7.1 Basic TypeScript Integration

Let's create a profile in CucumberJS that can connect our TypeScript files to CucumberJS when it runs. First, run `npm install ts-node --save-dev` to add `ts-node` to your development dependencies.

</> Example #49: Integrating TypeScript with Cucumber

```javascript
module.exports = {
    default: [
        '--require-module ts-node/register',
        '--require ./features/**/*.ts',
    ].join(' '),
};
```

Now, instead of writing step definitions in `.js` files, we'll use `.ts` files.

```typescript
import { Given } from '@cucumber/cucumber';
import { performLogin } from '../../src/session';

Given('the user {string} logs in', async function(user: string): Promise<void> {
    await performLogin(user);
});
```

10.7.2 Using cucumber-tsflow

If you want to use TypeScript for your step definitions while having a development experience more like CucumberJVM or SpecFlow, you can use the `cucumber-tsflow` library to add TypeScript decorators (similar to annotations) that you can use to decorate class methods and create step definitions.

To get started, run `npm install cucumber-tsflow`. You will also need to create or update `./features/tsconfig.json` to turn decorators on:

```json
{
    "compilerOptions": {
        "moduleResolution": "node",
        "experimentalDecorators": true
    }
}
```

</> Example #50: Writing TypeScript Step Definitions with Decorators

Now that TypeScript is configured and ready to use, let's write a step definition with `cucumber-tsflow`:

```typescript
import { binding, given } from 'cucumber-tsflow';
import { performLogin } from '../../src/session';

@binding()
export class Steps {

    @given('the user {string} logs in')
    public async givenTheUserLogsIn(user: string): Promise<void> {
        await performLogin(user);
    }
}
```

You can also create hooks and use tag expressions using decorators and even use dependency injection for loading custom `World` objects:

```typescript
import { binding, beforeAll, before, after, afterAll } from 'cucumber-tsflow';
import { CustomWorld } from '../CustomWorld';

@binding([CustomWorld])
export class Steps {
    public constructor(protected world: CustomWorld) {}

    @beforeAll()
    public static beforeAllTests(): void {
    }

    @before({ tag: '@sometag', timeout: 5000 })
    public beforeEachTest(): void {
    }

    @after()
    public afterEachTest(): void {
    }

    @afterAll()
    public static afterAllTest(): void {
    }
}
```

You may find this approach particularly appealing if you are supporting applications written in TypeScript, C#, and/or Java since the overall aesthetic is similar. For additional information about `cucumber-tsflow`,[111] refer to the documentation.

⚠ **Pitfall:** While TypeScript looks like Java or C#, it is still running on top of JavaScript, which **is not** a statically typed object-oriented language. TypeScript adds compile-time safety to JavaScript; however, you can still experience runtime errors that are simply not possible with true static typing.

---

[111] https://github.com/timjroberts/cucumber-js-tsflow

Chapter 11: Interacting with Systems

In this chapter, we will explore integrating Cucumber with your application's systems at different levels of integration starting with databases, and then the service and UI layers.

11.1 Integrating with Databases

 **Key Terms:**

> **Object Relational Mapper** - A software library that provides an abstraction layer between a database and an application by mapping the data stored in tables to objects within the application's code and vice versa.

It was mentioned in **Chapter 2** that using Cucumber for component testing is feasible in some cases. If a significant amount of your application's business logic is incorporated within database queries and your application uses an ORM, you can perform additional testing on these queries directly. Keep in mind that using an ORM is a design decision about how the application itself is built, so this approach is not feasible if an application wasn't already built with this type of design.

</> Example #51: Integrating an ORM with Cucumber

In this example we will connect to an in-memory SQLite database and create a "User" table. We will also load a new database and refresh the data for each scenario. Keep in mind that the ORM will need to be utilized by your application's code in order to benefit from integrating it with Cucumber.

◇ Ruby

ActiveRecord[112] is a popular ORM in Ruby. To get started, run `gem install activerecord sqlite3`.

Assuming your application has a file `./src/db/schema.rb`:

```ruby
require 'active_record'

class User < ActiveRecord::Base
end

def db_create_schema
    ActiveRecord::Schema.define do
        create_table :users, force: true do |t|
            t.string :name
            t.timestamps
        end
    end
end
```

---

[112]https://rubygems.org/gems/activerecord

Also assuming your application has a file `./src/db/connect.rb`:

```ruby
require 'active_record'

def db_connect
    # connect to the real database.
    ActiveRecord::Base.establish_connection(
        adapter: 'mysql',
        database: '...'
    )
end
```

Next, we need to write code to initialize an in-memory version of the database and load baseline test data. Create a file `./features/utils/db.rb`:

```ruby
require './src/db/schema'

def test_db_connect
    ActiveRecord::Base.establish_connection(
        adapter: 'sqlite3',
        database: ':memory:'
    )
end

def test_db_load_baseline
    User.create(name: 'Test User 1')
end
```

Set up Cucumber hooks that will create a new database for each scenario in `./features/support/db.rb`:

```ruby
require_relative '../utils/db'

test_db_connect

Before do
    db_create_schema
    test_db_load_baseline
end
```

Now you can use an ORM in your step definitions. Create a file `./features/step_definitions/db.rb`:

```ruby
require 'rspec'

Given('a user is created with name {string}') do |name|
    User.create!(name: name)
end

Then('a user with name {string} should exist') do |expected_name|
    user = User.find_by(name: expected_name)
    expect(user).not_to be_nil
    expect(user.name).to eq(expected_name)
end
```

🏅 **Pro Tip:** Consider loading your database configuration using your test configuration file. In a later example we'll look at how to implement this.

 Java

jOOQ[113] is a popular ORM for Java. To get started, update your `./pom.xml`:

```xml
<dependency>
    <groupId>org.jooq</groupId><artifactId>jooq</artifactId>
    <version>3.19.4</version>
</dependency>
<dependency>
    <groupId>org.xerial</groupId><artifactId>sqlite-jdbc</artifactId>
    <version>3.45.1.0</version>
</dependency>
```

Assuming your application has code to create a schema:

```java
import org.jooq.*;
import org.jooq.impl.*;
import static org.jooq.impl.DSL.*;

public class DBSchema {
    public static void createSchema(DSLContext context) {
        context.createTableIfNotExists("users")
                .column("id", SQLDataType.INTEGER.identity(true))
                .column("name", SQLDataType.VARCHAR(255))
                .constraints(constraint("PK_USERS").primaryKey("id")).execute();
    }
}
```

Create a file `./src/test/java/<Pkg Path>/db/DBTestUtils.java`:

```java
import org.jooq.*;
import org.jooq.impl.*;
import static org.jooq.impl.DSL.*;

public class DBTestUtils {
    public static DSLContext connect() { return DSL.using("jdbc:sqlite::memory:"); }

    public static void loadBaselineData(DSLContext context) {
        context.insertInto(table("users"), field("name"))
                .values("Test User 1").execute();
    }
}
```

You'll also need to add some additional code to your `CustomWorld` class.

```java
import org.jooq.DSLContext;

public class CustomWorld {
    private DSLContext context;
    public DSLContext getDBContext() {
        if (context == null) {
            context = DBTestUtils.connect();
            DBSchema.createSchema(context);
            DBTestUtils.loadBaselineData(context);
        }
        return context;
    } // ...existing code...
}
```

---

[113] https://jooq.org

Finally, you can create step definitions that make use of the ORM.

```java
import io.cucumber.java.en.*;
import org.jooq.Record;
import static org.jooq.impl.DSL.*;
import static org.junit.jupiter.api.Assertions.*;

public class UserSteps {
    private CustomWorld world;

    public UserSteps(CustomWorld world) {
        this.world = world;
    }

    @Given("a user is created with name {string}")
    public void aUserIsCreatedWithName(String name) {
        world.getDBContext().insertInto(table("users"), field("name"))
                .values(name)
                .execute();
    }

    @Then("a user with name {string} should exist")
    public void aUserWithNameShouldExist(String expectedName) {
        Record record = world.getDBContext().selectFrom(table("users"))
                                .where(field("name").eq(expectedName))
                                .fetchOne();
        assertEquals(expectedName, record.getValue(field("name"), String.class));
    }
}
```

JavaScript

Knex.js is a popular ORM for NodeJS. To get started, run `npm install knex sqlite3`.

Assuming your application has a file `./src/db.js`:

```javascript
const knex = require('knex');

let db = null;

function getDbContext() {
    if (!db) { db = knex({ client: 'mysql', connection: '...' }); }
    return db;
}

function setDbContext(context) { return (db = context); }

async function createSchema(context) {
    await context.schema.dropTableIfExists('users');
    await context.schema.createTable('users', (table) => {
        table.increments('id');
        table.string('name');
        table.timestamps(true, true);
    });
    return context;
}

module.exports = { getDbContext, setDbContext, createSchema };
```

Create a file `./features/utils/db.js`:

```javascript
const knex = require('knex');
const { setDbContext, createSchema } = require('../../src/db');

async function initializeDatabase() {
    const con = setDbContext(knex({ client: 'sqlite3', connection: ':memory:' }));
    return createSchema(con);
}

async function loadBaselineData(context) {
    await context('users').insert({ name: 'Test User 1' });
}

module.exports = { initializeDatabase, loadBaselineData };
```

Set up your hooks in `./features/support/db.js`:

```javascript
const { Before, After } = require('@cucumber/cucumber');
const { initializeDatabase, loadBaselineData } = require('../utils/db');

Before(async function hook() {
    this.db = await initializeDatabase();
    await loadBaselineData(this.db);
});
After(async function hook() { await this.db.destroy(); });
```

Finally, you can create step definitions that make use of the ORM:

```javascript
const { Given, Then } = require('@cucumber/cucumber');
const assert = require('assert');

Given('a user is created with name {string}', async function step(name) {
    await this.db('users').insert({ name });
});

Then('a user with name {string} should exist', async function step(name) {
    const user = await this.db('users').where('name', name).first();
    assert.strictEqual(user?.name, name);
});
```

</> Example #52: Utilizing Test Configuration with an ORM

Let's extend the previous example to use your test configuration.

◇ Ruby

In your test configuration file:

```yaml
db:
    adapter: 'sqlite3'
    database: ':memory:'
```

Update the file `./features/utils/db.rb`:

```ruby
def test_db_connect
    ActiveRecord::Base.establish_connection(Settings.db.to_h)
end
```

Java

In your test configuration file:

```
db: 'jdbc:sqlite::memory:'
```

Update the file `./src/test/java/<Pkg Path>/db/DBTestUtils.java`:

```java
public class DBTestUtils {
    // ...existing code...
    public static DSLContext connect(String config) {
        return DSL.using(config);
    }
}
```

Also update `CustomWorld`:

```java
public class CustomWorld {
    private DSLContext context;
    private Config config;

    public CustomWorld() {
        String env = System.getenv("TEST_ENV");
        this.config = ConfigFactory.load(env != null ? env : "default");
    }

    public DSLContext getDBContext() {
        if (context == null) {
            context = DBTestUtils.connect(this.config.getString("db"));
            DBSchema.createSchema(context);
            DBTestUtils.loadBaselineData(context);
        }
        return context;
    } // ...existing code...
}
```

JavaScript

In your test configuration file:

```
db:
    client: sqlite3
    connection: ':memory:'
```

Update the `./features/utils/db.js` file:

```javascript
const config = require('config');
const knex = require('knex');
const { setDbContext, createSchema } = require('../../src/db');

async function initializeDatabase() {
    const context = setDbContext(knex(config.db));
    return createSchema(context);
}
```

11.2 Integrating with Message Brokers

Another type of system that your applications may depend on is a message broker, which manages queues and topics that allow you to exchange messages across distributed components. Examples of message brokers include RabbitMQ,[114] Azure Service Bus,[115] and ActiveMQ.[116] These types of systems have become more popular because of microservice architectures.

 **Key Terms:**

> **Queue** - A messaging channel where messages are processed in First in, First out (FIFO) order. An individual message can only be received once.

> **Topic** - A messaging channel that allows messages to be published and then distributed to one or more subscribers. An individual message can be sent to multiple receivers.

11.2.1 Setting Up RabbitMQ

If you want to run your own RabbitMQ instance, you can download and run the `rabbitmq` Docker image:[117]

```
docker run -d --name rabbit --network devops \
  -p 5672:5672 -p 15672:15672 rabbitmq:latest
```

⚠ **Caution:** If you installed Report Portal from **Chapter 9**, you may have a conflict since it also creates a RabbitMQ Docker container.

11.2.2 Testing Message Broker Queues

Now that you have a running RabbitMQ instance, let's take a look at how to integrate a message broker with Cucumber.

</> **Example #53:** Integrating Message Broker Queues into Cucumber

The following examples can be tested with this scenario:

```
@rabbitmq
Scenario: Testing a Message Queue
When a message "hello!" is sent to the queue "messages"
Then the last message received is "hello!"
```

---

[114]https://rabbitmq-website.pages.dev/
[115]https://azure.microsoft.com/en-us/products/service-bus
[116]https://activemq.apache.org/
[117]https://hub.docker.com/_/rabbitmq

🔷 Ruby

You can use the bunny[118] gem to interact with RabbitMQ. To get started, run `gem install bunny`. Create `./features/support/messaging.rb`:

```ruby
require 'bunny'
require './src/messaging'

messaging_start

at_exit do
    messaging_stop
end

Before('@rabbitmq') do
    @connection = Bunny.new
    @connection.start
    @channel = @connection.create_channel
end

After('@rabbitmq') { @connection.close }
```

Assuming your application has a file `./src/messaging.rb`:

```ruby
require 'bunny'

Connection = Bunny.new

def messaging_start
    Connection.start
    channel = Connection.create_channel
    queue = channel.queue('messages')
    queue.subscribe do |delivery_info, properties, body|
        $last_message = body
        puts "---- Received #{body}"
    end
end

def messaging_stop
    return unless Connection.open?

    Connection.close
end
```

Also create a file `./features/step_definitions/messaging.rb`:

```ruby
require 'rspec'

When('a message {string} is sent to the queue {string}') do |message, queue_name|
    queue = @channel.queue(queue_name)
    queue.publish(message)
end

Then('the last message received is {string}') do |message|
    expect($last_message).to eq(message)
end
```

🛑 **Danger: Oh no...** the *Then* step fails! This type of problem is called a race condition and is a common timing problem in multithreaded

---

[118]https://rubygems.org/gems/bunny

applications. This happens because the message being received by the queue doesn't get processed until after the assertion is performed in the *Then* step. Use the `retries` gem from **8.1.2** to address this issue:

```ruby
require('rspec')
require('retries')

Then('the last message received is {string}') do |message|
    with_retries(
        max_tries: 10,
        rescue: [RSpec::Expectations::ExpectationNotMetError],
        base_sleep_seconds: 0.1,
        max_sleep_seconds: 2.0
    ) do
        expect($last_message).to eq(message)
    end
end
```

Subsequent examples will make use of retries to prevent a race condition.

Java

Add RabbitMQ client[119] to your `./pom.xml`:

```xml
<dependency>
    <groupId>com.rabbitmq</groupId><artifactId>amqp-client</artifactId>
    <version>5.20.0</version>
</dependency>
```

Assuming your application has a `MessagingService` class:

```java
import com.rabbitmq.client.*;

public class MessagingService {
    private Connection conn;
    private Channel channel;
    private String lastMessage = "";

    public void start() throws Exception {
        ConnectionFactory factory = new ConnectionFactory();
        factory.setHost("localhost");
        conn = factory.newConnection();
        channel = conn.createChannel();
        channel.queueDeclare("messages", false, false, true, null);
        channel.basicConsume("messages", true, (consumerTag, delivery) -> {
            lastMessage = new String(delivery.getBody(), "UTF-8");
            System.out.println("---- Received " + lastMessage);
        }, consumerTag -> { });
    }

    public void stop() throws Exception {
        if (conn != null && conn.isOpen()) { conn.close(); }
    }

    public String getLastMessage() { return lastMessage; }
}
```

---

[119]https://mvnrepository.com/artifact/com.rabbitmq/amqp-client

Let's set up a lazy loaded connection in your `CustomWorld` class:

```java
import com.rabbitmq.client.*;

public class CustomWorld {
    private Channel channel;
    // ... existing code ...

    public Channel getChannel() throws Exception {
        return getChannel(true);
    }

    public Channel getChannel(boolean isLazyLoad) throws Exception {
        if (channel == null && isLazyLoad) {
            ConnectionFactory factory = new ConnectionFactory();
            factory.setHost("localhost");
            Connection connection = factory.newConnection();
            channel = connection.createChannel();
        }
        return channel;
    }
}
```

Next, create a file `./src/test/java/<Pkg Path>/MessagingHooks.java`:

```java
import com.rabbitmq.client.Channel;
import io.cucumber.java.*;

public class MessagingHooks {
    private final CustomWorld world;
    private static MessagingService service;

    public MessagingHooks(CustomWorld world) {
        this.world = world;
    }

    public static MessagingService getMessaging() {
        return service;
    }

    @BeforeAll
    public static void beforeAll() throws Exception {
        service = new MessagingService();
        service.start();
    }

    @AfterAll
    public static void afterAll() throws Exception {
        service.stop();
    }

    @After
    public void afterScenario() throws Exception {
        Channel channel = this.world.getChannel(false);
        if (channel != null && channel.getConnection().isOpen()) {
            channel.getConnection().close();
        }
    }
}
```

⚠ **Caution:** In this example, we're initializing the `MessagingService` within the test startup/shutdown for convenience. In a real-world integration test, you may want to initialize your entire application instead of piece by piece, or your application may be assumed to be initialized and running elsewhere.

⚠ **Pitfall:** You can send messages to a queue, but do not intercept queue messages through your tests. Your application won't be able to receive messages if you "steal" the messages from the queue, which could affect the behavior of your application. Consider using a topic instead.

Let's also set up the step definitions that can send messages through a queue. In Ruby, we saw how a race condition can form when testing distributed systems such as message brokers. Use the Failsafe package[120] to manage retries in `./src/test/java/<Pkg Path>/MessagingSteps.java`:

```java
import com.rabbitmq.client.Channel;
import dev.failsafe.*;
import io.cucumber.java.en.*;
import java.time.Duration;
import java.time.temporal.ChronoUnit;
import static org.junit.jupiter.api.Assertions.*;

public class MessagingSteps {
    private final CustomWorld world;

    public MessagingSteps(CustomWorld world) {
        this.world = world;
    }

    @When("a message {string} is sent to the queue {string}")
    public void a_message_is_sent_to_queue(String message, String queueName)
        throws Exception {
        Channel channel = world.getChannel();
        channel.basicPublish("", queueName, null, message.getBytes());
    }

    @Then("the last message received is {string}")
    public void the_last_message_received_is(String message) throws Exception {
        RetryPolicy<Object> retryPolicy = RetryPolicy.builder()
                .withMaxRetries(10)
                .withDelay(Duration.ofSeconds(1))
                .withBackoff(100, 2000, ChronoUnit.MILLIS)
                .build();
        Failsafe.with(retryPolicy).run(() -> {
            String actual = MessagingHooks.getMessaging().getLastMessage();
            assertEquals(message, actual);
        });
    }
}
```

🏅 **Pro Tip:** The RabbitMQ client above is lazy loaded, so the use of scenario tag **@rabbitmq** is recommended but not required. However, it will be required in a future Java example when using topics.

⚠ **Caution:** The Failsafe library used above is different from the Failsafe Maven plugin mentioned in earlier sections. For the purposes of avoiding confusion, any reference to the Maven plugin will include the word Maven to distinguish it from the Java library used in this example.

---

[120] https://failsafe.dev/

📜 **JavaScript**

You can use amqplib[121] to communicate with RabbitMQ over AMQP. To get started, run `npm install amqplib`.

Assuming your application has a file `./src/messaging.js`:

```javascript
const amqp = require('amqplib');

let connection = null;
let channel = null;
let lastMessage = null;

async function connectMessaging() {
    connection = await amqp.connect('amqp://localhost');
    channel = await connection.createChannel();
    await channel.assertQueue('messages', { durable: false });

    await channel.consume('messages', (msg) => {
        lastMessage = msg.content.toString();
        console.log('---- Received ', lastMessage);
        channel.ack(msg);
    });

    return { connection, channel };
}

async function closeMessaging() {
    if (!connection) { return; }
    await connection.close();
}

const getLastMessage = () => lastMessage;

module.exports = { connectMessaging, closeMessaging, getLastMessage };
```

Create a file `./features/support/messaging.js`:

```javascript
const amqp = require('amqplib');
const { Before, After, BeforeAll, AfterAll } = require('@cucumber/cucumber');
const { connectMessaging, closeMessaging } = require('../../src/messaging');

BeforeAll(async () => {
    await connectMessaging();
});

AfterAll(async () => {
    await closeMessaging();
});

Before({ tags: '@rabbitmq' }, async function hook() {
    this.amqp = { connection: await amqp.connect('amqp://localhost') };
    this.amqp.channel = await this.amqp.connection.createChannel();
});

After({ tags: '@rabbitmq' }, async function hook() {
    if (!this.amqp?.connection) { return; }
    await this.amqp.connection.close();
});
```

---

[121] https://www.npmjs.com/package/amqplib

⚠ **Caution:** Similar to the previous Java example, we're initializing application messaging within the test startup/shutdown for convenience.

Also create a file for step definitions so you can send messages to a queue. You can use the promise-retry package[122] to avoid the race condition issues from earlier. In `./features/step_definitions/messaging.js`:

```javascript
const { When, Then } = require('@cucumber/cucumber');
const { getLastMessage } = require('../../src/messaging');
const assert = require('assert');
const promiseRetry = require('promise-retry');

When('a message {string} is sent to the queue {string}', async function (msg, q) {
    await this.amqp.channel.sendToQueue(q, Buffer.from(msg));
});

Then('the last message received is {string}', function (expectedMessage) {
    return promiseRetry(async function (retry) {
        try {
            assert.strictEqual(getLastMessage(), expectedMessage);
        } catch (ex) { retry(); }
    }, {
        retries: 10,
        factor: 2,
        minTimeout: 100,
        maxTimeout: 2000,
    });
});
```

11.2.3 Testing Message Broker Topics

In the previous example, we connected to RabbitMQ using an AMQP client and sent messages into the queue so that we could trigger behaviors in the application under test. Message brokers also provide topics, which allow multiple subscribers to receive messages that are sent to them. Let's extend our code from the previous example to subscribe to one or more topics, and then listen for incoming messages on those topics.

</> Example #54: Integrating Message Broker Topics into Cucumber

The following examples can be run with the following scenario:

```gherkin
@rabbitmq
Scenario: Sending and Receiving Topics
When a message "hello!" is sent to the topic "topic_messages"
Then a message "hello!" should be received by the topic "topic_messages"
```

---

[122]https://www.npmjs.com/package/promise-retry

Let's update the file `./features/support/messaging.rb`:

```ruby
# ...existing code...

Before('@rabbitmq') do
    @connection = Bunny.new
    @connection.start
    @channel = @connection.create_channel
    @topic_exchange = @channel.topic('topic_exchange', auto_delete: true)
    @topic_messages = []
    queue = @channel
            .queue('', exclusive: true)
            .bind(@topic_exchange, routing_key: '#')
    queue.subscribe do |delivery_info, properties, body|
        @topic_messages << { body: body, topic: delivery_info.routing_key }
        puts "---- Topic #{delivery_info.routing_key}: #{body}"
    end
end
```

Also add new steps to `./features/step_definitions/messaging.rb`:

```ruby
require 'retries'
# ...existing code...
When('a message {string} is sent to the topic {string}') do |message, topic|
    @topic_exchange.publish(message, routing_key: topic)
end

Then('a message {string} should be received by the topic {string}') do |msg, t|
    with_retries(
        max_tries: 10,
        rescue: [RSpec::Expectations::ExpectationNotMetError],
        base_sleep_seconds: 0.1,
        max_sleep_seconds: 2.0
    ) do
        msgs = @topic_messages
                .select { |m| m[:topic] == t }
                .map { |m| m[:body] }
        expect(msgs).to include(msg)
    end
end
```

☕ **Java**

First, let's make some changes to `CustomWorld`:

```java
import java.util.*;

public class CustomWorld {
    private HashMap<String, ArrayList<String>> topicMessages = new HashMap<>();
    // ...existing code...

    public void addTopicMessage(String topic, String message) {
        topicMessages.computeIfAbsent(topic, k -> new ArrayList<>()).add(message);
    }

    public List<String> getTopicMessages(String topic) {
        return topicMessages.getOrDefault(topic, new ArrayList<>());
    }
}
```

There are also changes to **MessagingHooks**:

```java
import com.rabbitmq.client.*;
import io.cucumber.java.*;

public class MessagingHooks {
    // ...existing code...
    private DeliverCallback onTopicMessage() {
        return (consumerTag, delivery) -> {
            String message = new String(delivery.getBody(), "UTF-8");
            String topic = delivery.getEnvelope().getRoutingKey();
            world.addTopicMessage(topic, message);
            System.out.println(String.format("---- Topic %s: %s", topic, message));
        };
    }

    @Before("@rabbitmq")
    public void beforeScenario() throws Exception {
        Channel channel = this.world.getChannel();
        channel.exchangeDeclare("topic_exchange", BuiltinExchangeType.TOPIC);
        String q = channel.queueDeclare().getQueue();
        channel.queueBind(q, "topic_exchange", "#");
        channel.basicConsume(q, true, onTopicMessage(), consumerTag -> { });
    }

    @After("@rabbitmq")
    public void afterScenario() throws Exception {
        // ...existing code...
    }
}
```

Finally, add the new step definitions to **MessagingSteps**. We'll also use the
Failsafe library from **Chapter 8** to handle retries:

```java
import com.rabbitmq.client.Channel;
import dev.failsafe.*;
import io.cucumber.java.en.*;
import java.time.Duration;
import java.time.temporal.ChronoUnit;
import static org.junit.jupiter.api.Assertions.*;

public class MessagingSteps {
    // ...existing code...
    @When("a message {string} is sent to the topic {string}")
    public void a_message_is_sent_to_topic(String msg, String t)
        throws Exception {
        world.getChannel().basicPublish("topic_exchange", t, null, msg.getBytes());
    }

    @Then("a message {string} should be received by the topic {string}")
    public void a_message_should_be_received_by_topic(String msg, String t)
        throws Exception {
        RetryPolicy<Object> retryPolicy = RetryPolicy.builder()
                .withMaxRetries(10)
                .withDelay(Duration.ofSeconds(1))
                .withBackoff(100, 2000, ChronoUnit.MILLIS)
                .build();
        Failsafe.with(retryPolicy).run(() -> {
            assertTrue(world.getTopicMessages(t).contains(msg));
        });
    }
}
```

📜 **JavaScript**:

Update the file `./feature/support/messaging.js`:

```javascript
const { Before } = require('@cucumber/cucumber');
const amqp = require('amqplib');

// ...existing code...

Before({ tags: '@rabbitmq' }, async function () {
    const connection = await amqp.connect('amqp://localhost');
    this.amqp = { connection, topics: {} };
    this.amqp.channel = await this.amqp.connection.createChannel();

    await this.amqp.channel.assertExchange('topic_exchange', 'topic', {
        durable: false
    });

    const q = await this.amqp.channel.assertQueue('', { exclusive: true });
    await this.amqp.channel.bindQueue(q.queue, 'topic_exchange', '#');
    await this.amqp.channel.consume(q.queue, (msg) => {
        const topicName = msg.fields.routingKey;
        this.amqp.topics[topicName] = this.amqp.topics[topicName] || [];
        this.amqp.topics[topicName].push(msg.content.toString());
        console.log(`---- Topic ${topicName}: ${msg.content.toString()}`);
    }, { noAck: true });
});
// ...existing code...
```

Also update `./feature/step_definitions/messaging.js`:

```javascript
const { When, Then } = require('@cucumber/cucumber');
const promiseRetry = require('promise-retry');
const assert = require('assert');

// ...existing code...

When('a message {string} is sent to the topic {string}', async function (msg, t) {
    await this.amqp.channel.publish('topic_exchange', t, Buffer.from(msg));
});

Then('a message {string} should be received by the topic {string}', function (m, t) {
    return promiseRetry((retry) => {
        try {
            assert.ok(this.amqp?.topics?.[t]);
            assert.ok(this.amqp.topics[t].includes(m));
        } catch (ex) { retry(); }
    }, {
        retries: 10,
        factor: 2,
        minTimeout: 100,
        maxTimeout: 2000,
    });
});
```

🎖️ **Pro Tip:** Use your test configuration or scenario tags to configure which topics need to be subscribed to when your scenarios run. The above examples are simple demonstrations and, ideally in a large test suite, there shouldn't be anything hard-coded into the setup functions. You may also want to share the AMQP connection across scenarios to improve performance, but then you would have to manage test isolation yourself.

11.3 Performing HTTP-based API Testing

So far, we've discussed the concept of performing testing against HTTP-based APIs without a specific implementation. In this section, we'll take a look at how to integrate an HTTP client into Cucumber so that you can build and extend your integration testing to include service APIs.

11.3.1 Leveraging Existing Libraries

It is possible to use existing libraries for performing HTTP calls; however, there are significant limitations that need to be considered.

◈ Ruby

You can use the `cucumber-rest-bdd` gem,[123] which has pre-built steps for testing HTTP-based service APIs. However, this library only supports Cucumber Ruby 3, so consider implementing your own HTTP steps instead.

▣ Java

Unfortunately, there is no pre-built HTTP step library for CucumberJVM. In the next section, we'll look at how to build one yourself.

▤ JavaScript

For CucumberJS, you can use the `cucumber-steps-api` NPM package,[124] which has pre-built steps for testing HTTP-based service APIs. Unfortunately, this package is hard-coded to depend on CucumberJS 4. Even if the package had used a peer dependency,[125] CucumberJS has changed package names as of version 7. Consider implementing your own HTTP steps.

11.3.2 Making HTTP Calls Directly

Making HTTP requests from Cucumber will be similar regardless of which programming language you're using: You'll need to set up an HTTP client library, and create a common function that your steps can use to initiate the HTTP call. In the following examples, you'll create a function (or method) called `executeHttpRequestInternal`, which will serve as the core function for your HTTP steps. You will also create a function `executeHttpRequest` with additional Cucumber-based functionality. This design allows for easy mocking for testing your steps' behavior, makes the code within your step definitions simple, and allows for upgrading and changing the underlying HTTP client in the future. Consider adding timeouts and retries to these functions to improve the reliability and performance of your tests.

---

[123] https://github.com/graze/cucumber-rest-bdd
[124] https://www.npmjs.com/package/cucumber-steps-api
[125] https://nodejs.org/en/blog/npm/peer-dependencies

</> Example #55: Integrating an HTTP Client Library

In this example, we'll look at how to build a wrapper around an HTTP client, with support for recording requests and responses as well as control over handling errors at the scenario and test runner level. Then, we'll look at how to integrate this code into Cucumber. By default, an HTTP status code of 400 or greater will throw an error unless the "http.ignoreErrors" configuration setting is set to **true** or the **@http-ignore-errors** scenario tag is attached to the scenario or feature being run.

◇ Ruby

Create a file **./features/utils/HttpTest.rb**:

```ruby
module HttpTest
    @requests = []
    @responses = []
    @ignore_errors = false

    def add_request(request)
        @requests.unshift(request)
    end

    def add_response(response)
        @responses.unshift(response)
    end

    def get_requests
        @requests
    end

    def get_responses
        @responses
    end

    def get_ignore_errors
        @ignore_errors
    end

    def set_ignore_errors(val)
        @ignore_errors = val
    end

    def reset
        @ignore_errors = false
        @requests = []
        @responses = []
    end

    module_function :add_request
    module_function :add_response
    module_function :get_requests
    module_function :get_responses
    module_function :get_ignore_errors
    module_function :set_ignore_errors
    module_function :reset
end
```

This is a Ruby module that can be utilized in other parts of the code.

Next, create a file: `./features/support/http.rb`:

```ruby
require 'uri'
require 'net/http'
require 'json'
require './features/utils/HttpTest'

def execute_http_request_internal(url:, method: 'GET', headers: {}, body: nil)
    uri = URI.parse(url)
    http = Net::HTTP.new(uri.host, uri.port)
    http.use_ssl = uri.scheme == 'https'

    request_class = Net::HTTP.const_get(method.capitalize)
    request = request_class.new(uri)

    request.body = body.to_json if %w[POST PUT PATCH].include?(method.upcase) && body

    headers.each { |key, value| request[key] = value }

    http.request(request)
rescue NameError
    raise "Unsupported HTTP method: #{method}"
end

def execute_http_request(request)
    url = "#{Settings.http.baseUrl}#{request[:url]}"
    ignore_errors = HttpTest.get_ignore_errors || Settings.http.ignoreErrors
    HttpTest.add_request(request)
    res = execute_http_request_internal(
        url: url,
        method: request[:method],
        headers: request[:headers],
        body: request[:body]
    )
ensure
    HttpTest.add_response(res)
    raise "HTTP Error: #{res.code} #{res.message}" if !ignore_errors &&
                                                       res.code.to_i >= 400

    res
end

Before('@http-ignore-errors') do
    HttpTest.set_ignore_errors(true)
end

After do
    HttpTest.reset
end
```

Finally, you can perform HTTP calls from within Ruby step definitions and evaluate the results.

```ruby
Given('an HTTP {string} call {string} is made') do |method, url|
    execute_http_request({
                            url: url,
                            method: method,
                            headers: {},
                            body: nil
                         })
end
```

Since Java is a statically typed language, unlike Ruby and JavaScript, the CucumberJVM implementation will have more model classes and object mapping between types to provide separation from the underlying HTTP client implementation.

Create a file `./src/test/java/<Pkg Path>/http/HttpRequest.java`:

```java
import java.util.HashMap;
import java.util.Map;

public class HttpRequest {
    private String baseUrl = "";
    private final String url;
    private final String method;
    private final String body;
    private final String bodyType;
    private final Map<String, String> headers;

    public HttpRequest(String url, String method, String body) {
        this(url, method, body, null, null);
    }

    public HttpRequest(String url, String method, String body,
        Map<String, String> headers, String bodyType) {
        this.url = url;
        this.headers = headers != null ? headers : new HashMap<String,String>();
        this.method = method;
        this.body = body;
        this.bodyType = bodyType != null ? bodyType : "application/json";
    }

    public void setBaseUrl(String url) { this.baseUrl = url; }
    public String getUrl() { return baseUrl + url; }
    public String getMethod() { return method; }
    public String getBody() { return body; }
    public String getBodyType() { return bodyType; }
    public Map<String, String> getHeaders() { return headers; }
}
```

Create a file `./src/test/java/<Pkg Path>/http/HttpResponse.java`:

```java
import java.util.List;
import java.util.Map;

public class HttpResponse {
    private final int statusCode;
    private final String body;
    private final Map<String, List<String>> headers;

    public HttpResponse(int code, Map<String, List<String>> headers, String body) {
        this.statusCode = code;
        this.headers = headers;
        this.body = body;
    }

    public int getStatusCode() { return statusCode; }
    public boolean isSuccessful() { return statusCode >= 400; }
    public String getBody() { return body; }
    public Map<String, List<String>> getHeaders() { return headers; }
}
```

OKHttp[126] is a popular HTTP client for Java. Add it to `./pom.xml`:

```xml
<dependency>
    <groupId>com.squareup.okhttp3</groupId>
    <artifactId>okhttp</artifactId>
    <version>4.12.0</version>
    <scope>test</scope>
</dependency>
```

Then create file `./src/test/java/<Pkg Path>/http/HttpClient.java`:

```java
import com.typesafe.config.Config;
import okhttp3.*;
import java.io.IOException;
import java.util.Map;

public class HttpClient {
    private final OkHttpClient httpClient;
    private final CustomWorld world;
    private final Config config;

    public HttpClient(CustomWorld world, Config config) {
        this.httpClient = new OkHttpClient();
        this.world = world;
        this.config = config;
    }

    public HttpResponse executeHttpRequest(HttpRequest request) throws IOException {
        HttpResponse res = null;
        boolean httpIgnoreErrors = this.config.getBoolean("http.ignoreErrors") ||
            world.getHttpIgnoreErrors();
        request.setBaseUrl(this.config.getString("http.baseUrl"));
        this.world.addHttpRequest(request);
        try {
            res = executeHttpRequestInternal(request);
            System.out.println(res.isSuccessful());
            if (!res.isSuccessful() && !httpIgnoreErrors) {
                throw new IOException("HTTP " + res.getStatusCode() + ": " +
                    res.getBody());
            }
        } finally { this.world.addHttpResponse(res); }
        return res;
    }

    private HttpResponse executeHttpRequestInternal(HttpRequest req)
    throws IOException {
        Request.Builder requestBuilder = new Request.Builder()
                .url(req.getUrl()).method(req.getMethod(), req.getBody() != null ?
                    RequestBody.create(req.getBody(),
                        MediaType.parse(req.getBodyType())) : null);
        for (Map.Entry<String, String> entry : req.getHeaders().entrySet()) {
            requestBuilder.addHeader(entry.getKey(), entry.getValue());
        }
        Response response = httpClient.newCall(requestBuilder.build()).execute();
        try {
            return new HttpResponse(
                    response.code(), response.headers().toMultimap(),
                    response.body() != null ? response.body().string() : null
            );
        } finally { response.close(); }
    }
}
```

---

[126] https://square.github.io/okhttp/

You'll also need to add some additional code to your `CustomWorld` class:

```java
import java.util.ArrayList;
import java.util.List;

public class CustomWorld {
    private boolean httpIgnoreErrors = false;
    private List<HttpRequest> httpRequests = new ArrayList<HttpRequest>();
    private List<HttpResponse> httpResponses = new ArrayList<HttpResponse>();

    public List<HttpRequest> getHttpRequests() {
        return httpRequests;
    }

    public List<HttpResponse> getHttpResponses() {
        return httpResponses;
    }

    public void addHttpRequest(HttpRequest req) {
        httpRequests.add(0, req);
    }

    public void addHttpResponse(HttpResponse res) {
        httpResponses.add(0, res);
    }

    public boolean getHttpIgnoreErrors() {
        return httpIgnoreErrors;
    }

    public void setHttpIgnoreErrors(boolean value) {
        httpIgnoreErrors = value;
    }
}
```

Finally, you can make HTTP calls from your Java step definitions.

```java
import io.cucumber.java.en.Given;
import java.io.IOException;
import com.typesafe.config.*;

public class StepDefinitions {
    private CustomWorld world;
    private Config config;
    private HttpClient client;

    public StepDefinitions(CustomWorld world) {
        String env = System.getenv("TEST_ENV");
        this.world = world;
        this.config = ConfigFactory.load(env != null ? env : "default");
        this.client = new HttpClient(this.world, this.config);
    }

    @Before("@http-ignore-errors")
    public void before_http_ignore_errors() {
        world.setHttpIgnoreErrors(true);
    }

    @Given("an HTTP {string} call {string} is made")
    public void given_a_step_which_makes_an_http_call(String method, String url)
        throws IOException {
        this.client.executeHttpRequest(new HttpRequest(url, method, null));
    }
}
```

📜 JavaScript

Axios[127] is a popular HTTP client for NodeJS. To get started, run `npm install axios`. In a file `./features/utils/http.js`:

```javascript
const axios = require('axios');
const config = require('config');

async function executeHttpRequestInternal({
    url, method = 'GET', headers = {}, body = null }) {
    const response = await axios({
        method,
        url,
        headers,
        data: body
    });
    return response;
}

async function executeHttpRequest(world, request) {
    let res;
    world.http = world?.http ?? {};
    world.http.requests = world?.http?.requests ?? [];
    world.http.responses = world?.http?.responses ?? [];
    const ignoreErrors = world.http.ignoreErrors || config?.http?.ignoreErrors;
    try {
        const req = { ...request, url: `${config?.http?.baseUrl}${request.url}` };
        world.http.requests.unshift(req);
        res = await executeHttpRequestInternal(req);
    } catch (err) {
        if (!err.response || !ignoreErrors) {
            throw err;
        }
        res = err.response;
    } finally {
        world.http.responses.unshift(res);
    }
    return res;
}

module.exports = { executeHttpRequest };
```

Finally, you can make HTTP calls from JavaScript step definitions.

```javascript
const { Before, Given } = require('@cucumber/cucumber');
const { executeHttpRequest } = require('../../utils/http');


Before({ tags: '@http-ignore-errors' }, function () {
    this.http = this?.http ?? {};
    this.http.ignoreErrors = true;
});

Given('an HTTP {string} call {string} is made', async function(method, url) {
    const response = await executeHttpRequest(this, { method, url });
});
```

---

[127] https://www.npmjs.com/package/axios

🏅 **Pro Tip:** Consider implementing retries and timeouts from **Chapter 8** in `executeHttpRequest` so that your tests can be more resilient to transient failures. When you integrate retries, you can improve performance by only retrying HTTP 5xx and HTTP 429 errors.

</> Example #56: Validating HTTP Responses

Once you make HTTP calls, you will want to be available to validate the results of those calls. Let's look at an example feature file:

```gherkin
Feature: test feature

    @http-ignore-errors
    Scenario: scenario 1
    Given an HTTP "GET" call "/" is made
    Then the HTTP call should have returned an HTTP 401
```

💎 Ruby

You can use rspec to assert the HTTP responses that were captured.

```ruby
require 'rspec'

Then('the HTTP call should have returned an HTTP {int}') do |status|
    expect(HttpTest.get_responses[0].code).to eq(status.to_s)
end
```

🔳 Java

You can use JUnit to assert the HTTP responses that were captured.

```java
public class MySteps {
    @Then("the HTTP call should have returned an HTTP {int}")
    public void then_the_last_http_call_returned(int status) {
        int actual = world.getHttpResponses().get(0).getStatusCode();
        Assertions.assertEquals(status, actual);
    }
}
```

📜 JavaScript

You can use `assert` to assert the HTTP responses that were captured.

```javascript
const { Then } = require('@cucumber/cucumber');
const assert = require('assert');

Then('the HTTP call should have returned an HTTP {int}', function (status) {
    assert.strictEqual(this?.http?.responses?.[0]?.status, status);
});
```

🏅 **Pro Tip:** When recording HTTP requests and responses, add new items to the beginning of the list, so the first element is always the latest request or response. This will make your tests more intuitive to understand and avoid magic numbers.

11.4 Testing Web Browser UIs

In order to build end-to-end tests for a modern application, you will need
to be able to validate the behavior of your application's browser-based UIs.
In this section, we will look at some pre-built tools that can help you build
UI tests in Cucumber as well as explore building your own UI testing steps
using Selenium WebDriver with Cucumber.

11.4.1 Overview of Web Browser UI Testing

When you initiate a UI test, Selenium WebDriver will begin running a new
instance of the target web browser. Then your tests will be able to run
different operations against the web browser to trigger different behaviors
and validate the state of UI. Let's review the types of supported operations:

- **Browser Navigation** - You can navigate to a specific page, refresh
  the current page, or navigate forward or backwards.
- **Locate HTML Elements** - You can find elements by using a CSS
  selector or XPath, and then validate the state of those elements.
- **Click** - You can trigger DOM events on HTML elements such as
  clicking on them.
- **Send Keys** - You can type text into text fields on the screen.
- **Execute Scripts** - You can run client-side JavaScript code within
  the context of the page to run custom functionality.
- **Window Management** - Support for navigating IFrames, pop-up
  windows, and dialogues.
- **Cookie Management** - You can set and clear cookies within the
  browser.
- **Screenshots** - You can take a screenshot of the browser. This is
  useful for capturing the state of the UI when a scenario fails.

You can then combine these different operations to configure your UI test,
change the state of the UI to trigger a behavior, and then validate that
the behavior occurred as expected. Selenium also has support for all major
browsers, and can be used in "headless" mode where the browser is not
visible on the screen.

🏅 **Pro Tip:** If you want to run your UI tests across multiple browsers
without having to support the infrastructure yourself, consider using a Web-
Driver-compatible cloud-based service such as Sauce Labs or BrowserStack.
This is especially helpful if you need to test in browsers that cannot be
easily run on servers such as Safari.

</> Example #57: Simple Search Page

All examples in the next three sections will use the "Simple Search Page" application. To get started, run `npm install -g http-server`. Then create a directory and a file within it called `./index.html`:

```html
<!doctype html>
<html lang="en">
<head>
    <meta charset="UTF-8">
    <title>Simple Search Page</title>
    <script>
        function performSearch() {
            var searchInput = document.getElementById('search_box').value;
            var resultsArea = document.getElementById('results');
            if (searchInput.trim() !== '') {
                resultsArea.innerHTML = 'Results for: ' + searchInput;
            } else {
                resultsArea.innerHTML = 'Please enter a search query.';
            }
            return false;
        }
    </script>
</head>
<body>
    <h1>Simple Search Page</h1>
    <form onsubmit="return performSearch();">
        <input type="text" id="search_box" placeholder="Enter search query...">
        <input type="submit" value="Search">
    </form>
    <div id="results"></div>
</body>
</html>
```

Run `http-server -p 9999` in a terminal from the directory where your `index.html` is located. You can now use your browser to access the application at `http://localhost:9999`. The HTTP server must be running while your UI tests are running.

11.4.2 Using Selenium WebDriver Directly

While there are some newer web browser UI testing libraries such as Cypress, Playwright, and Puppeteer, Selenium has remained popular even after 20 years of existence. Let's create UI tests using Selenium directly. You can run this example with the following scenario:

```gherkin
@webdriver
Scenario: the user can search with a query with webdriver
    Given the homepage is opened with webdriver
    When "something" is typed into the search box with webdriver
    And the "Search" button is pressed with webdriver
    Then the results should display "Results for: something" with webdriver
```

⚠ **Caution:** When using Selenium WebDriver directly, you will need to handle your own retries for assertions. You are also responsible for directly managing the lifecycle of the WebDriver.

💎 Ruby

To get started, run `gem install selenium-webdriver` and create the file
`./features/support/webdriver.rb`:

```ruby
require 'selenium-webdriver'
Before('@webdriver') { @driver = Selenium::WebDriver.for :firefox }
After('@webdriver') { @driver.quit }
```

Then create the file `./features/step_definitions/webdriver.rb`:

```ruby
require 'rspec'

Given('the homepage is opened with webdriver') do
    @driver.navigate.to 'http://localhost:9999'
end

When('{string} is typed into the search box with webdriver') do |value|
    wait = Selenium::WebDriver::Wait.new(timeout: 10)
    wait.until { @driver.find_element(id: 'search_box').displayed? }
    element = @driver.find_element(id: 'search_box')
    element.send_keys(value)
end

When('the {string} button is pressed with webdriver') do |btn|
    path = "//input[@type='submit'][@value='#{btn}']"
    wait = Selenium::WebDriver::Wait.new(timeout: 10)
    wait.until { @driver.find_element(xpath: path).displayed? }
    button = @driver.find_element(xpath: path)
    button.click
end

Then('the results should display {string} with webdriver') do |results|
    wait = Selenium::WebDriver::Wait.new(timeout: 10)
    wait.until { @driver.find_element(id: 'results').displayed? }
    text = @driver.find_element(id: 'results').text
    expect(text).to eq(results)
end
```

☕ Java

To get started, update your `./pom.xml`:

```xml
<dependency>
    <groupId>org.seleniumhq.selenium</groupId><artifactId>selenium-java</artifactId>
    <version>4.18.0</version><scope>test</scope>
</dependency>
```

Create a file `./src/test/java/<Pkg Path>/WebDriverHooks.java`:

```java
import io.cucumber.java.After;

public class WebDriverHooks {
    private CustomWorld world;
    public WebDriverHooks(CustomWorld world) { this.world = world; }
    @After
    public void tearDown() {
        if (world.getDriver(false) != null) { world.getDriver().quit(); }
    }
}
```

Update `CustomWorld` to load WebDriver:

```java
import java.time.Duration;
import org.openqa.selenium.WebDriver;
import org.openqa.selenium.firefox.FirefoxDriver;
import org.openqa.selenium.support.ui.WebDriverWait;

public class CustomWorld {
    private WebDriver driver;
    private WebDriverWait wait;
    // ...existing code...
    public WebDriver getDriver() { return getDriver(true); }
    public WebDriver getDriver(boolean isLazyLoad) {
        if (driver == null && isLazyLoad) {
            driver = new FirefoxDriver();
        }
        return driver;
    }

    public WebDriverWait getWait() {
        if (wait == null) {
            wait = new WebDriverWait(getDriver(), Duration.ofSeconds(10));
        }
        return wait;
    }
}
```

Create a file `./src/test/java/<Pkg Path>/WebDriverSteps.java`:

```java
import io.cucumber.java.en.*;
import org.openqa.selenium.*;
import org.openqa.selenium.support.ui.ExpectedConditions;
import static org.junit.jupiter.api.Assertions.*;

public class WebDriverSteps {
    private CustomWorld world;
    public WebDriverSteps(CustomWorld world) { this.world = world; }

    @Given("the homepage is opened with webdriver")
    public void openHomepage() { world.getDriver().get("http://localhost:9999"); }

    @When("{string} is typed into the search box with webdriver")
    public void theUserFillsInTheSearchBoxWith(String value) {
        WebElement searchBox = world.getDriver().findElement(By.id("search_box"));
        searchBox.sendKeys(value);
    }

    @When("the {string} button is pressed with webdriver")
    public void theUserPresses(String btn) {
        WebElement submitButton = world.getDriver().findElement(
            By.cssSelector("input[type='submit'][value='" + btn + "']"));
        submitButton.click();
    }

    @Then("the results should display {string} with webdriver")
    public void theUserShouldSeeInTheResults(String expectedText) {
        WebElement results = world.getWait().until(
            ExpectedConditions.visibilityOfElementLocated(By.id("results")));
        assertTrue(results.getText().contains(expectedText));
    }
}
```

📜 JavaScript

To get started, run: `npm install selenium-webdriver --save-dev`

Create a file `./features/support/webdriver.js`:

```javascript
const { Before, After } = require('@cucumber/cucumber');
const { Builder } = require('selenium-webdriver');

Before({ tags: '@webdriver' }, async function () {
    this.driver = await new Builder().forBrowser('firefox').build();
});

After({ tags: '@webdriver' }, async function () {
    if (this.driver) {
        await this.driver.quit();
    }
});
```

Then create `./features/step_definitions/webdriver.js`:

```javascript
const { Given, When, Then } = require('@cucumber/cucumber');
const { By, until } = require('selenium-webdriver');
const assert = require('assert');

Given('the homepage is opened with webdriver', async function () {
    await this.driver.get('http://localhost:9999');
});

When('{string} is typed into the search box with webdriver', async function (text) {
    const input = await this.driver.findElement(By.css('input[type="text"]'));
    await input.sendKeys(text);
});

When('the {string} button is pressed with webdriver', async function (text) {
    const button = await this.driver.findElement(
        By.css(`input[type="submit"][value="${text}"]`));
    await button.click();
});

Then('the results should display {string} with webdriver', async function (text) {
    const results = await this.driver.wait(
        until.elementLocated(By.css('div#results')), 10000);
    const resultsText = await results.getText();
    assert.ok(resultsText.includes(text));
});
```

🏅 **Pro Tip:** Consider setting the test URL and browser configuration from your test configuration file.

11.4.3 Leveraging WebDriver Libraries

Building your own WebDriver integration can be complicated because of configuration, handling retries and timeouts, and managing page models. Using an abstraction to manage WebDriver can simplify your code and help make your tests more reliable.

 **Ruby**

Capybara[128] is a popular acceptance testing tool in Ruby that can be integrated with Cucumber. You will also use the Selenium WebDriver[129] gem. To get started, run: `gem install capybara selenium-webdriver`

You can run this example with the following scenario:

```
Scenario: the user can search with a query with capybara
    Given the homepage is opened with capybara
    When "something" is typed into the search box with capybara
    And the "Search" button is pressed with capybara
    Then the results should display "Results for: something" with capybara
```

Create a file `./features/support/capybara.rb`:

```ruby
require 'capybara/cucumber'
require 'selenium-webdriver'

Capybara.register_driver :selenium_firefox do |app|
    Capybara::Selenium::Driver.new(app, browser: :firefox)
end

Capybara.default_driver = :selenium_firefox
Capybara.app_host = 'http://localhost:9999'
```

Next, create a file `./features/step_definitions/capybara.rb`:

```ruby
require 'rspec'

Given('the homepage is opened with capybara') { visit('/') }

When('{string} is typed into the search box with capybara') do |value|
    fill_in 'search_box', with: value
end

When('the {string} button is pressed with capybara') do |btn|
    click_button(btn)
end

Then('the results should display {string} with capybara') do |results|
    expect(page).to have_selector('#results', text: results)
end
```

As you can see, much less code is required when using Capybara compared to integrating with Selenium WebDriver directly.

---

[128] https://teamcapybara.github.io/capybara/
[129] https://rubygems.org/gems/selenium-webdriver

⊟ Java

Selenide[130] provides an abstraction on top of WebDriver in Java and can also be integrated into CucumberJVM. You can run this example with the following scenario:

```
Scenario: the user can search with a query with selenide
    Given the homepage is opened with selenide
    When "something" is typed into the search box with selenide
    And the "Search" button is pressed with selenide
    Then the results should display "Results for: something" with selenide
```

To get started, update your `./pom.xml`:

```xml
<dependency>
    <groupId>com.codeborne</groupId><artifactId>selenide</artifactId>
    <version>7.1.0</version><scope>test</scope>
</dependency>
```

Create a file `./src/test/java/<Pkg Path>/SelenideHooks.java`:

```java
import com.codeborne.selenide.Configuration;
import io.cucumber.java.BeforeAll;

public class SelenideHooks {
    @BeforeAll
    public static void setup() {
        Configuration.browser = "firefox";
    }
}
```

Create a file `./src/test/java/<Pkg Path>/SelenideSteps.java`:

```java
import io.cucumber.java.en.*;
import static com.codeborne.selenide.Selenide.*;
import static com.codeborne.selenide.Condition.*;

public class SelenideSteps {
    @Given("the homepage is opened with selenide")
    public void theUserIsOnTheHomepage() {
        open("http://localhost:9999");
    }
    @When("{string} is typed into the search box with selenide")
    public void theUserFillsInTheSearchBoxWith(String value) {
        $("#search_box").setValue(value);
    }
    @When("the {string} button is pressed with selenide")
    public void theUserPresses(String btn) {
        $$("input[type='submit']").findBy(value(btn)).click();
    }

    @Then("the results should display {string} with selenide")
    public void theUserShouldSeeInTheResults(String expectedText) {
        $("#results").shouldHave(text(expectedText));
    }
}
```

---

[130] https://selenide.org/

📜 JavaScript

WebdriverIO[131] is a popular WebDriver library for JavaScript. To get started, run:

```
npm install webdriverio wdio-geckodriver-service --save-dev
```

You can run this example with the following scenario:

```gherkin
@webdriverio
Scenario: the user can search with a query with webdriverio
    Given the homepage is opened with webdriverio
    When "something" is typed into the search box with webdriverio
    And the "Search" button is pressed with webdriverio
    Then the results should display "Results for: something" with webdriverio
```

Create a file `./features/support/webdriverio.js`:

```javascript
const { Before, After } = require('@cucumber/cucumber');
const { remote } = require('webdriverio');

Before({ tags: '@webdriverio', timeout: 60000 }, async function () {
    this.driverio = await remote({
        logLevel: 'warn',
        capabilities: { browserName: 'firefox' }
    });
});

After({ tags: '@webdriverio' }, async function () {
    if (this.driverio) { await this.driverio.deleteSession(); }
});
```

Then create a file `./features/step_definitions/webdriverio.js`:

```javascript
const { Given, When, Then } = require('@cucumber/cucumber');
const assert = require('assert');

Given('the homepage is opened with webdriverio', async function () {
    await this.driverio.url('http://localhost:9999');
});

When('{string} is typed into the search box with webdriverio', async function (val) {
    const input = await this.driverio.$('input[type="text"]');
    await input.setValue(val);
});

When('the {string} button is pressed with webdriverio', async function (text) {
    const button = await this.driverio.$(`input[type="submit"][value="${text}"]`);
    await button.click();
});

Then('the results should display {string} with webdriverio', async function (text) {
    const results = await this.driverio.$('div#results');
    await results.waitForDisplayed({ timeout: 10000 });
    const resultsText = await results.getText();
    assert.ok(resultsText.includes(text));
});
```

---

[131] https://webdriver.io

11.4.4 Web Browser UI Testing with Playwright

Playwright[132] is a new UI testing library from Microsoft that does not use Selenium WebDriver. It can also be used with Java, .NET, and others. You can run these examples with the following scenario:

```
@playwright
Scenario: the user can search with a query with playwright
    Given the homepage is opened with playwright
    When "something" is typed into the search box with playwright
    And the "Search" button is pressed with playwright
    Then the results should display "Results for: something" with playwright
```

💎 Ruby

Unfortunately, there is not yet a Playwright client written for Ruby.

☰ Java

To get started, update your `./pom.xml`:

```xml
<dependency>
    <groupId>com.microsoft.playwright</groupId><artifactId>playwright</artifactId>
    <version>1.41.2</version><scope>test</scope>
</dependency>
```

Update your `CustomWorld`:

```java
import com.microsoft.playwright.*;

public class CustomWorld {
    //...existing code...
    private static Playwright playwright = Playwright.create();
    private Page page;

    public Page getPage() {
        if (page == null) {
            Browser browser = playwright.firefox().launch();
            page = browser.newPage();
        }
        return page;
    }
    //...existing code...
}
```

---

[132]https://playwright.dev/

Next, create a file `./src/test/java/<Pkg Path>/PlaywrightHooks.java`:

```java
import io.cucumber.java.After;

public class PlaywrightHooks {
    private CustomWorld world;
    public PlaywrightHooks(CustomWorld world) {
        this.world = world;
    }

    @After("@playwright")
    public void afterPlaywright() {
        world.getPage().context().browser().close();
    }
}
```

Finally, create a file `./src/test/java/<Pkg Path>/PlaywrightSteps.java`:

```java
import com.microsoft.playwright.*;
import io.cucumber.java.en.*;
import static org.junit.jupiter.api.Assertions.assertTrue;

public class PlaywrightSteps {
    private CustomWorld world;

    public PlaywrightSteps(CustomWorld world) {
        this.world = world;
    }

    @Given("the homepage is opened with playwright")
    public void theHomepageIsOpenedWithPlaywright() {
        world.getPage().navigate("http://localhost:9999");
    }

    @When("{string} is typed into the search box with playwright")
    public void stringIsTypedIntoTheSearchBoxWithPlaywright(String query) {
        world.getPage().fill("input[type='text']", query);
    }

    @When("the {string} button is pressed with playwright")
    public void theButtonIsPressedWithPlaywright(String text) {
        world.getPage().click(
            String.format("input[type='submit'][value='%s']", text));
    }

    @Then("the results should display {string} with playwright")
    public void theResultsShouldDisplayWithStringWithPlaywright(String text) {
        ElementHandle resultsDiv = world.getPage().waitForSelector("div#results");
        assertTrue(resultsDiv.textContent().contains(text));
    }
}
```

📜 JavaScript

To get started, run `npm install playwright` and then you'll also need to run `npx playwright install` to set up additional files.

🏅 **Pro Tip:** Playwright runs in headless mode by default, so when you execute your tests you will not see a browser appear, and the tests will run faster than the Selenium-based tests you've seen so far.

Create a file `./features/support/playwright.js`:

```javascript
const { Before, After } = require('@cucumber/cucumber');
const { firefox } = require('playwright');

Before({ tags: '@playwright' }, async function hook() {
    this.browser = await firefox.launch();
    this.page = await this.browser.newPage();
});

After({ tags: '@playwright' }, async function hook() {
    if (this.browser) {
        await this.browser.close();
    }
});
```

Then create a file `./features/step_definitions/playwright.js`:

```javascript
const { Given, When, Then } = require('@cucumber/cucumber');
const assert = require('assert');
const url = 'http://localhost:9999';

Given('the homepage is opened with playwright', async function () {
    await this.page.goto(url);
});

When('{string} is typed into the search box with playwright', async function (text) {
    await this.page.fill('input[type="text"]', text);
});

When('the {string} button is pressed with playwright', async function (text) {
    await this.page.click(`input[type="submit"][value="${text}"]`);
});

Then('the results should display {string} with playwright', async function (text) {
    await this.page.waitForSelector('div#results');
    assert.ok((await this.page.textContent('div#results')).includes(text));
});
```

11.4.5 WebDriver Client Click and Send Keys

If you are using Selenium WebDriver directly, you can use the
`executeScript` command to create client-side implementations for
`click` and `sendKeys`, which can be useful for more complex testing
situations. For example, the native `click` doesn't always work correctly
when too many layered elements are close together, and for some browsers,
the native `sendKeys` implementation can be slow.

◇ Ruby

```ruby
def client_click(driver, css)
    code = 'document.querySelector(arguments[0]).click();'
    driver.execute_script(code, css)
end

def client_sendkeys(driver, css, val)
    code = 'document.querySelector(arguments[0]).value = arguments[1];'
    driver.execute_script(code, css, val)
end
```

▣ Java

```java
public class WebDriverUtils {
    public static void clientClick(WebDriver driver, String css) {
        ((JavascriptExecutor) driver).executeScript(
            "document.querySelector(arguments[0]).click();", css);
    }

    public static void clickSendKeys(WebDriver driver, String css, String val) {
        ((JavascriptExecutor) driver).executeScript(
            "document.querySelector(arguments[0]).value = arguments[1];", css, val);
    }
}
```

▤ JavaScript

```javascript
async function clientClick(driver, css) {
    const code = 'document.querySelector(arguments[0]).click();';
    await driver.executeScript(code, css);
}

async function clientSendKeys(driver, css, val) {
    const code = 'document.querySelector(arguments[0]).value = arguments[1];';
    await driver.executeScript(code, css, val);
}
```

🏅 **Pro Tip:** You can use this same technique to send events other than
`click` to HTML elements in the DOM.

11.5 Testing Mobile UIs

Besides browser-based UIs, many applications also have a mobile UI for Android or iOS devices. In this section, we'll install the tools required to run Android apps and use Appium to write automated tests for one.

11.5.1 Installing Appium and Android

Before using Appium to perform testing on the mobile app, you'll need to set up the required tools:

- Android Studio[133]
- Appium Server:[134] run `npm install appium -g`
- Appium Inspector[135]

1) Open Android Studio, configure for standard settings. It will then download the required emulators and tools.

2) In Android Studio, go to "More Actions" > "SDK Manager" menu item. Copy the "Android SDK Path" and create a system-wide environment variable ANDROID_HOME for the copied path.

3) In Android Studio, click "More Actions" > "Virtual Device Manager" menu item. Note the name of the emulated device and the Android version (located underneath the name), then press "start" (play icon). The emulator should now be visible and running.

4) In a terminal, run `appium driver install uiautomator2`. Then run `appium` to start the Appium server. **You will need to keep this program running** while using Appium Inspector or running tests.

5) You can test your configuration by downloading an APK file and entering the following JSON into App Inspector once it's running:

```
{
    "platformName": "android",
    "platformVersion": "<device version from Virtual Device Manager>",
    "deviceName": "<device name from Virtual Device Manager>",
    "automationName": "UiAutomator2",
    "app": "<path to your APK file>"
}
```

After clicking the "Start Session" button, your app should be running in the emulator, and you should also be able to inspect its components.

---

[133] https://developer.android.com/studio
[134] https://www.npmjs.com/package/appium
[135] https://github.com/appium/appium-inspector/releases

11.5.2 Testing an Android App

</> Example #58: Testing the MyDemoApp Android App

You'll be running your tests against the Sauce labs My Demo App.[136] Download the APK file and copy it to `./bin/MyDemoApp.apk` in your Cucumber project. You can run this example with the following scenario:

```
@mobile
Scenario: the user can see the shopping cart
    Given the app is opened
    When the "cart badge" is clicked
    Then the "cart screen" should be displayed
```

♢ Ruby

To get started, run `gem install appium_lib`. Add the following properties to your `settings.yml` file for `ruby-config`:

```
mobile:
  appium:
    caps:
      platformName: android
      platformVersion: '<device version from Virtual Device Manager>'
      deviceName: <device name from Virtual Device Manager>
      app: ./bin/MyDemoApp.apk
      automationName: UiAutomator2
    appium_lib:
      server_url: http://localhost:4723
  mydemoapp:
    cart badge: //android.view.ViewGroup[@content-desc="cart badge"]
    cart screen: //android.widget.ScrollView[@content-desc="cart screen"]
```

Create a file `./features/support/mobile.rb`:

```ruby
require 'appium_lib'

Before('@mobile') do
    proj = File.expand_path('../..', __dir__)
    caps = Settings.mobile.appium.to_h.deep_symbolize_keys
    caps[:caps][:app] = File.join(proj, Settings.mobile.appium.caps.app)
    @appium = Appium::Driver.new(caps, true)
    Appium.promote_appium_methods Object
end

After('@mobile') { @appium.driver_quit }

class MyDemoApp
    def initialize(appium)
        @appium = appium
    end

    def find_element(name)
        @appium.find_element(:xpath, Settings.mobile.mydemoapp[name])
    end
end
```

🏅 **Pro Tip:** The `MyDemoApp` class is acting as a page model.

---

[136] https://github.com/saucelabs/my-demo-app-rn/releases

Finally, create a file `./features/step_definitions/mobile.rb`:

```ruby
require 'rspec'

Given('the app is opened') do
    @appium.start_driver
    @mydemoapp = MyDemoApp.new(@appium)
end

When('the {string} is clicked') do |item|
    wait = Selenium::WebDriver::Wait.new(timeout: 10)
    element = wait.until { @mydemoapp.find_element(item) }
    element.click
end

Then('the {string} should be displayed') do |item|
    wait = Selenium::WebDriver::Wait.new(timeout: 10)
    wait.until do
        found_element = @mydemoapp.find_element(item)
        found_element if found_element.displayed?
    end
end
```

You should now be able to run the mobile app scenario successfully.

 **Java**

Add Appium and Selenium WebDriver to your `./pom.xml`:

```xml
<dependency>
    <groupId>org.seleniumhq.selenium</groupId><artifactId>selenium-java</artifactId>
    <version>4.18.0</version><scope>test</scope>
</dependency>
<dependency>
    <groupId>io.appium</groupId><artifactId>java-client</artifactId>
    <version>9.1.0</version><scope>test</scope>
</dependency>
```

🏅 **Pro Tip:** Appium is based on Selenium and uses the same WebDriver technology. Consider writing code common to both types of tests.

Assuming you are using `com.typesafe.config` from **10.1**, Add a property "mobile" to `./src/test/resources/default.json`:

```json
{
    "appium": {
        "serverUrl": "http://localhost:4723",
        "caps": {
            "platformVersion": "<device version from Virtual Device Manager>",
            "deviceName": "<device name from Virtual Device Manager>",
            "app": "./bin/MyDemoApp.apk",
            "platformName": "android",
            "automationName": "UiAutomator2"
        }
    },
    "mydemoapp": {
        "cart badge": "//android.view.ViewGroup[@content-desc=\"cart badge\"]",
        "cart screen": "//android.widget.ScrollView[@content-desc=\"cart screen\"]"
    }
}
```

Add additional code to **CustomWorld**:

```java
import com.typesafe.config.*;
import io.appium.java_client.AppiumDriver;
import org.openqa.selenium.remote.DesiredCapabilities;

public class CustomWorld {
    private Config config;
    private AppiumDriver appium;
    private MyDemoApp app;
    public CustomWorld() {
        String env = System.getenv("TEST_ENV");
        this.config = ConfigFactory.load(env != null ? env : "default");
    } // ...existing code...

    public AppiumDriver getAppium() {
        if (appium == null) {
            Config capsConfig = config.getConfig("mobile.appium.caps");
            DesiredCapabilities c = new DesiredCapabilities();
            for (Map.Entry<String, ConfigValue> e : capsConfig.entrySet()) {
                String v = capsConfig.getString(e.getKey());
                if ("app".equals(e.getKey())) {
                    try {
                        c.setCapability(e.getKey(), new File(v).getCanonicalPath());
                    } catch (IOException ex) { c.setCapability(e.getKey(), v); }
                } else { c.setCapability(e.getKey(), v); }
            }
            try {
                appium = new AppiumDriver(
                    new URL(config.getString("mobile.appium.serverUrl")), c);
            } catch (Exception e) { throw new RuntimeException(e); }
        }
        return appium;
    }

    public MyDemoApp getMyDemoApp() {
        if (app == null) {
            app = new MyDemoApp(getAppium(), config.getConfig("mobile.mydemoapp"));
        }
        return app;
    } // ...existing code...
}
```

Next, create a new class **MyDemoApp**:

```java
import com.typesafe.config.Config;
import io.appium.java_client.AppiumDriver;
import org.openqa.selenium.*;
import org.openqa.selenium.support.ui.*;

public class MyDemoApp {
    private final AppiumDriver appium;
    private final Config config;

    public MyDemoApp(AppiumDriver appium, Config config) {
        this.appium = appium;
        this.config = config;
    }

    public WebElement findElement(String name) {
        String xpath = config.getString(name);
        return new WebDriverWait(appium, Duration.ofSeconds(10))
                .until(ExpectedConditions.presenceOfElementLocated(By.xpath(xpath)));
    }
}
```

Create a file `./src/test/java/<Pkg Path>/MobileHooks.java`:

```java
import io.cucumber.java.*;

public class MobileHooks {
    private CustomWorld world;

    public MobileHooks(CustomWorld world) {
        this.world = world;
    }

    @Before("@mobile")
    public void beforeMobile() {
        world.getMyDemoApp();
    }

    @After("@mobile")
    public void afterMobile() {
        world.getAppium().quit();
    }
}
```

Finally, create a file `./src/test/java/<Pkg Path>/MobileSteps.java`:

```java
import io.cucumber.java.en.*;
import java.time.Duration;
import org.openqa.selenium.WebElement;
import org.openqa.selenium.support.ui.*;

public class MobileSteps {
    private final CustomWorld customWorld;

    public MobileSteps(CustomWorld customWorld) {
        this.customWorld = customWorld;
    }

    @Given("the app is opened")
    public void theAppIsOpened() {
        customWorld.getMyDemoApp();
    }

    @When("the {string} is clicked")
    public void theElementIsClicked(String item) {
        WebElement element = customWorld.getMyDemoApp().findElement(item);
        element.click();
    }

    @Then("the {string} should be displayed")
    public void theElementShouldBeDisplayed(String item) {
        WebElement element = customWorld.getMyDemoApp().findElement(item);
        new WebDriverWait(customWorld.getAppium(), Duration.ofSeconds(10))
            .until(ExpectedConditions.visibilityOf(element));
    }
}
```

You should now be able to run the mobile app scenario successfully.

📜 JavaScript

To get started, run `npm install appium --save-dev`. Using the `config` package, add the following to your configuration file:

```
mobile:
  appium:
    port: 4723
    logLevel: warn
    capabilities:
      appium:platformName: android
      appium:platformVersion: '<device version from Virtual Device Manager>'
      appium:deviceName: <device name from Virtual Device Manager>
      appium:automationName: UiAutomator2
      appium:app: ./bin/MyDemoApp.apk
  mydemoapp:
    cart badge: //android.view.ViewGroup[@content-desc="cart badge"]
    cart screen: //android.widget.ScrollView[@content-desc="cart screen"]
```

Create a file `./features/support/mobile.js`:

```javascript
const { Before, After } = require('@cucumber/cucumber');
const { remote } = require('webdriverio');
const config = require('config');
const path = require('path');

Before({ tags: '@mobile', timeout: 60000 }, async function () {
    const capabilities = config?.mobile?.appium?.capabilities;
    const appFile = path.join(process.cwd(), capabilities['appium:app']);
    capabilities['appium:app'] = appFile;

    this.mydemoapp = config?.mobile?.mydemoapp;
    this.appium = await remote({
        ...config?.mobile?.appium,
        capabilities
    });
});

After({ tags: '@mobile' }, async function () {
    if (this.appium) { await this.appium.deleteSession(); }
});
```

Finally, create a file `./features/step_definitions/mobile.js`:

```javascript
const { Given, When, Then } = require('@cucumber/cucumber');
const assert = require('assert');

Given('the app is opened', async function () { /* noop */ });

When('the {string} is clicked', async function (item) {
    const element = await this.appium.$(this.mydemoapp[item]);
    await element.click();
});

Then('the {string} should be displayed', async function (item) {
    const element = await this.appium.$(this.mydemoapp[item]);
    assert.ok(await element.isDisplayed());
});
```

You should now be able to run the mobile app scenario successfully.

11.6 Scaling Out UI Testing with Selenium Grid

Performing web browser and mobile UI testing requires more CPU and memory than other forms of testing, so running these types of tests at scale through CI/CD pipelines requires additional infrastructure. To allow for scaling, you can use Selenium Grid. In this section, you'll use Docker to run your UI test automation through a worker node on Selenium Grid.

11.6.1 Setting Up Selenium Grid

</> Example #59: Running Selenium Grid with Docker

First, start a Selenium Grid hub using the `selenium/hub` Docker image.[137] This will serve as the nexus of communication between the worker nodes:

```
docker run -d --name selenium-hub --network devops \
  -p 4442-4444:4442-4444 \
  selenium/hub
```

In a browser, navigate to `http://localhost:4444/ui` to review the status of Selenium Grid. Next, initialize a worker node with the Firefox web browser using the `selenium/node-firefox` Docker image:[138]

```
docker run -d --name selenium-firefox-node-1 --network devops \
  -e SE_EVENT_BUS_HOST=selenium-hub \
  -e SE_EVENT_BUS_PUBLISH_PORT=4442 \
  -e SE_EVENT_BUS_SUBSCRIBE_PORT=4443 \
  selenium/node-firefox
```

After starting the node, confirm that it is visible in the Selenium Grid UI.

⚠ **Caution:** There is a Selenium plugin for Jenkins;[139] however, it hasn't been updated since 2019 and it has a known security vulnerability CVE-2020-2196.[140] If you use this plugin to manage your Selenium Grid, take appropriate precautions to ensure that you avoid a CSRF attack.

11.6.2 Using WebDriver with Selenium Grid

</> Example #60: Simple Search Page Revisited

In this section, we'll be modifying your UI tests from **11.4.2**. As a reminder, you must run an HTTP server on port 9999, which hosts the `./index.html` file, while running your UI tests or they will not behave as expected.

---

[137]https://hub.docker.com/r/selenium/hub
[138]https://hub.docker.com/r/selenium/node-firefox
[139]https://plugins.jenkins.io/selenium/
[140]https://nvd.nist.gov/vuln/detail/CVE-2020-2196

💎 Ruby

Make changes to `./features/step_definitions/webdriver.rb`:

```ruby
Given('the homepage is opened with webdriver') do
    @driver.navigate.to 'http://host.docker.internal:9999'
end
```

⚠️ **Pitfall:** For Windows and macOS, the `host-docker.internal` DNS entry is enabled by default within Docker. On Linux, you'll have to set it manually when you call `docker run` using the `--add-host=host.docker.internal:host-gateway` flag.

Also update `./features/support/webdriver.rb`:

```ruby
require 'selenium-webdriver'

Before('@webdriver') do
    options = Selenium::WebDriver::Firefox::Options.new
    @driver = Selenium::WebDriver.for(
        :remote,
        url: 'http://localhost:4444/wd/hub',
        capabilities: options
    )
end
# ...existing code...
```

Your existing UI test should now run against the Selenium Grid.

🗐 Java

You'll need to make updates to `getDriver()` in `CustomWorld`:

```java
public class CustomWorld {
    // ...existing code...
    public WebDriver getDriver(boolean isLazyLoad) {
        if (driver == null && isLazyLoad) {
            try {
                FirefoxOptions options = new FirefoxOptions();
                Url url = new URL("http://localhost:4444/wd/hub");
                driver = new RemoteWebDriver(url, options);
            } catch (MalformedURLException e) { throw new RuntimeException(e); }
        }
        return driver;
    }
}
```

Also change the `Given` step in `WebDriverSteps` with the new URL:

```java
public class WebDriverSteps {
    // ...existing code...
    @Given("the homepage is opened with webdriver")
    public void theUserIsOnTheHomepage() {
        world.getDriver().get("http://host.docker.internal:9999");
    }
}
```

Your existing UI test should now run against the Selenium Grid.

📜 JavaScript

Update `./features/support/webdriver.js`:

```javascript
const { Before, After } = require('@cucumber/cucumber');
const { Builder } = require('selenium-webdriver');

Before({ tags: '@webdriver' }, async function () {
    this.driver = await new Builder().forBrowser('firefox')
        .usingServer('http://localhost:4444/wd/hub').build();
}); // ...existing code...
```

Also update `./features/step_definitions/webdriver.js`:

```javascript
const { Given } = require('@cucumber/cucumber');

Given('the homepage is opened with webdriver', async function () {
    await this.driver.get('http://host.docker.internal:9999');
}); // ...existing code...
```

🏅 **Pro Tip:** Consider storing browser type, capabilities configurations, and the URL to your application in your test configuration file instead of directly in code. In a real-world development environment, you will have many configurations that your tests will need to be able to support.

11.6.3 Using WebDriver Libraries with Selenium Grid

In **11.4.4**, we also looked at using libraries that provide abstractions above WebDriver for performing automated UI testing. Let's see how we can integrate these into Selenium Grid as well.

💎 Ruby

You can reconfigure Capybara to connect to Selenium Grid instead of a local WebDriver. To get started, modify `./features/support/capybara.rb`:

```ruby
require 'capybara/cucumber'
require 'selenium-webdriver'

Capybara.register_driver :selenium_remote do |app|
    Capybara::Selenium::Driver.new(app,
                                   browser: :remote,
                                   url: 'http://localhost:4444/wd/hub',
                                   desired_capabilities: :firefox)
end
Capybara.default_driver = :selenium_remote
Capybara.app_host = 'http://host.docker.internal:9999'
```

Your existing UI test should now run against the Selenium Grid.

☕ Java

Selenide can also be reconfigured to use Selenium Grid.

Update the file `./src/test/java/<Pkg Path>/SelenideHooks.java`:

```java
public class SelenideHooks {
    @BeforeAll
    public static void setup() {
        Configuration.remote = "http://localhost:4444/wd/hub";
        Configuration.browser = "firefox";
    }
}
```

Also update `./src/test/java/<Pkg Path>/SelenideSteps.java`:

```java
public class SelenideSteps {
    @Given("the homepage is opened with selenide")
    public void theUserIsOnTheHomepage() {
        open("http://host.docker.internal:9999");
    } // ...existing code...
}
```

JavaScript

Make changes to `./feature/support/webdriverio.js`:

```javascript
const { Before } = require('@cucumber/cucumber');
const { remote } = require('webdriverio');

Before({ tags: '@webdriverio', timeout: 60000 }, async function () {
    this.driverio = await remote({
        logLevel: 'warn',
        hostname: 'localhost', port: 4444, path: '/wd/hub',
        capabilities: { browserName: 'firefox' }
    });
}); // ...existing code...
```

Also change `./features/step_definitions/webdriverio.js`:

```javascript
const { Given } = require('@cucumber/cucumber');
Given('the homepage is opened with webdriverio', async function () {
    await this.driverio.url('http://host.docker.internal:9999');
}); // ...existing code...
```

11.6.4 Using Playwright with Selenium Grid

Playwright has experimental support for Selenium Grid; however, it only
works with Google Chrome and Microsoft Edge browsers. To run your Playwright tests on Selenium Grid, set the `SELENIUM_REMOTE_URL` environment
variable to `http://<selenium grid address>:4444` and then run tests.

11.6.5 Using Appium with Selenium Grid

It is possible to run mobile UI testing across a Selenium Grid with Appium;
however, the setup and configuration is complex and specific to your testing
requirements. Running emulators on Docker is not recommended because it
lacks the recommended hardware acceleration capabilities.

11.7 Avoiding Step Definition Confusion

Now that we've looked at how to write HTTP-based API tests as well as web browser and mobile UI tests, let's take a look at how to avoid confusion in your test suite. Consider the following Gherkin step:

```
Given the user "Jimmy" logs into the app
```

How do you know which implementation it is using? Is it initiating a WebDriver session and manipulating a browser, or perhaps it's calling an OAuth API to acquire a token for the given user? Since Gherkin is meant to separate the technical from the nontechnical parts of managing and implementing business rules for software, it's the job of the programmer to resolve the confusion here. In this section, we'll look at some different ways to solve this problem and consider the pros and cons of each approach.

11.6.1 Separate Projects

The simplest way of avoiding confusion between API and UI steps is to simply have two different projects so that the API and UI tests are physically separate. This approach is simple to understand and easy to implement; however, your step definitions are less reusable because they cannot be shared.

11.6.2 Step Definition Prefix or Suffix

One solution is to add a prefix or suffix to your steps such as:

```
Feature: API and UI testing\index{ui testing} example

    Scenario: An API-based test
    Given [API] the user "Jimmy" logs into the app
    # ...

    Scenario: A UI-based test
    Given [UI] the user "Jimmy" logs into the app
    # ...
```

This will help avoid confusion about the underlying implementation of a step. This approach also allows you to quickly convert an API test to a UI test and vice versa.

Pros

- Simple to read and understand for technical people.
- Supports mixing API-based and UI-based steps into a single scenario.
- Existing API tests can be copied and "converted" to UI tests, and vice versa.

Cons

- All step definitions will need to abide by this standard. Also, this approach would need to be implemented at the beginning of a project.
- This may be confusing for nontechnical people.
- Including technical specifics directly in the step definition name can reduce the effectiveness of your feature files as documentation.

11.6.3 Scenario Tags

Another solution involves using scenario tags such as `@api` or `@ui` to indicate to the affected step definitions which implementation to use. For example:

```
Feature: API and UI testing\index{ui testing} example

Scenario Outline: A test which can do both
Given the user "<User>" logs into the app
# ...

@api
Examples:
| User  |
| Jimmy |

@ui
Examples:
| User  |
| Jimmy |
```

This approach gives Cucumber a way of determining the difference between implementations without bringing attention to it directly in the step itself.

Pros

- Simple to read and understand for technical people while being out of the way for nontechnical people.
- Possible to support both API and UI versions of a scenario without copy/pasting by using a scenario outline with two examples with each one having its own scenario tags.
- This approach can be implemented on existing step definitions because it doesn't depend on the step definition name.

Cons

- An individual scenario is either an API or UI test, so steps cannot be mixed between the two.
- This implementation requires more development effort and is more complicated than other approaches.
- If you are using step libraries, both API- and UI-based steps will need to be in the same step library since both implementations are "sharing" a step definition.

Chapter 12: Utilizing Patterns

Software design patterns are well-known and reliable general solutions to common problems in software. Let's review some patterns that can help you to keep your growing tests organized and sensible.

12.1 Using Dependency Injection

Back in **6.4.2**, you learned how to use dependency injection to provide a shared `CustomWorld` instance across all of your step definitions and hooks in Java. You also implemented a `World` module in Ruby using `World()` and a `CustomWorld` class in JavaScript using `setWorldConstructor`. These are all different forms of dependency injection.

 **Key Terms:**

> **Dependency Injection** - A design pattern in software development where the dependencies of a component are injected into it rather than it creating or managing the dependencies itself. This approach allows for loose coupling between components, making the code more modular, testable, and maintainable.

> **Interface** - In statically typed languages such as Java and C#, refers to an abstract type that acts as a contract by requiring specific methods to be present in any classes that claim to implement that type. This language feature allows for different implementations of the same interface to be interchangeable, while allowing the compiler to properly enforce types.

12.2.1 Types of Dependency Injection

Constructor Injection   This type involves the use of arguments to a class constructor to inject dependencies. PicoContainer uses this approach to inject `CustomWorld` into your step and hook class constructors.

Setter Injection   This type involves calling a setter function to specify the object being injected. Both Cucumber for Ruby and CucumberJS use this approach to dependency injection for setting up the `World` modules or class respectively.

Interface Injection   In both constructor and setter injection, there may be cases where the implementation of a dependency needs to be resolved at runtime. For example, if your application interacts with a database, you may want to use an in-memory implementation of your database for testing and then a different implementation for actually running your application. With statically typed languages such as Java, this means that the injected dependency will need to be an interface.

12.2.2 Using a Dependency Injection Library

</> Example #61: Instantiating an API Service Component

◇ Ruby

Injectable[141] is a Ruby gem that includes mix-ins for defining injectable dependencies in Ruby classes. To get started, run `gem install injectable`. For example:

```ruby
class UsersService
    include Injectable
    dependency :http
    dependency :message_broker
    argument :url
end
```

▤ Java

Previously, we used PicoContainer to inject dependencies into class constructors. Guice[142] is another library that can be used to load dependencies. To get started, update your `./pom.xml` file:

```xml
<dependency>
    <groupId>com.google.inject</groupId><artifactId>guice</artifactId>
    <version>7.0.0</version>
</dependency>
```

For example the `UserService` class:

```java
import com.google.inject.*;

public class UsersService {
    private final HttpService httpService;
    private final MessageBrokerService messageBrokerService;
    private final String url;

    @Inject
    public UsersService(
        HttpService http, MessageBrokerService mb, @Named("url") String url) {
        this.httpService = http;
        this.messageBrokerService = mb;
        this.url = url;
    }
}
```

▤ JavaScript

Typically, JavaScript and NodeJS code doesn't use dependency injection libraries because the language itself is so dynamic that such a design pattern can be implemented directly in the code. However, if you are using TypeScript, consider using TypeDI.[143]

---

[141] https://github.com/rubiconmd/injectable
[142] https://github.com/google/guice
[143] https://github.com/typestack/typedi

12.2 Using Singletons

Another software design pattern that is often used with Cucumber is the singleton. In earlier examples, we created objects within the scenario context that would exist for the duration of a scenario. In some cases, we may want to create an object that can exist for the entire test run. For example, you may want to use the same WebDriver instance for all scenarios.

 **Key Terms:**

> **Singleton** - A design pattern in software development in which a component exists as a single instance that can be accessed from anywhere within an application.

 **Example #62:** Creating a Singleton Class

 **Ruby**

Since Ruby has global variables, the need for singletons is debatable. However, you can use the singleton[144] gem to implement one using a mix-in:

```ruby
require 'singleton'

class TestHelpers
    include Singleton

    # ... your code here...
end
```

Java

Implementing a singleton in Java requires creating a **static** field and method on your class. Also, add a private constructor so that the class cannot be instantiated directly:

```java
public class TestHelpers {
    private static TestHelpers instance;

    private TestHelpers() { }

    public static TestHelpers getInstance() {
        if (instance == null) {
            instance = new TestHelpers();
        }
        return instance;
    }

    // ... your code here...
}
```

Caution: This implementation of a lazy-loaded singleton is sufficient for a single-threaded application; however, if you have multiple threads running, this singleton will behave unpredictably.

---

[144]https://github.com/ruby/singleton

Instead, use a double-checked lock to ensure that only one thread can instantiate the underlying instance:

```java
public class TestHelpers {
    private static TestHelpers instance;

    private TestHelpers() { }

    public static TestHelpers getInstance() {
        if (instance == null) {
            synchronized (TestHelpers.class) {
                if (instance == null) {
                    instance = new TestHelpers();
                }
            }
        }
        return instance;
    }

    // ... your code here...
}
```

JavaScript

In NodeJS or JavaScript with modules, any variable at the top-level scope of a file that is accessible either directly or through a getter function can be considered a singleton. While there are no private constructors in JavaScript, you can prevent a class from being instantiated directly by simply not exporting it so it won't be available. This approach is reliable in NodeJS because the runtime environment is single-threaded, and only the first call to **require** or **import** will execute the code being included, with all subsequent calls being cached:

```javascript
class TestHelpers {
    // ... your code here...
}

let instance = null;
function getTestHelpers() {
    if (instance === null) {
        instance = new TestHelpers();
    }
    return instance;
}

module.exports = { getTestHelpers };
```

Anti-pattern: JavaScript also has global variables, but using them in most cases is considered an anti-pattern. Most linters and code checkers will display an error if one is being used. Instead, use module exports to manage your singleton objects.

Pro Tip: If you're using TypeScript, you can use the same approach as in Java to implement a singleton with a private constructor and a lazy-loaded getter function. Since TypeScript is ultimately running on the NodeJS runtime, it is still single-threaded, so no locking is required.

12.3 Using Page Object Models

In **11.5**, you used a test configuration file to store a mapping between the name of a component in an Android app and the XPath required to access it. You can extend this approach to create model classes that represent each page of your application. This is called a Page Object model.

12.3.1 Implementing Page Object Models Directly

</> Example #63: Page Object Models for Simple Search Page

In the following example, we are going to revisit the code from **11.4.2**. In each language, the initialization of **SimpleSearchPage** will be implemented differently to demonstrate different approaches to managing pages.

◇ Ruby

You can implement a Page Object model in Ruby by building a class. In this example, **SimpleSearchPage** will be instantiated by the Gherkin step that navigates to the page. To get started, create a file **./features/pages/SimpleSearchPage.rb**:

```ruby
require 'selenium-webdriver'

class SimpleSearchPage
    def initialize(driver, base_url)
        @driver = driver
        @url = "#{base_url}/index.html"
        @search_box_locator = { id: 'search_box' }
        @results_locator = { id: 'results' }
    end

    def open
        @driver.navigate.to @url
    end

    def type_search(query)
        wait = Selenium::WebDriver::Wait.new(timeout: 10)
        wait.until { @driver.find_element(@search_box_locator).displayed? }
        search_box = @driver.find_element(@search_box_locator)
        search_box.clear
        search_box.send_keys(query)
    end

    def submit_search
        wait = Selenium::WebDriver::Wait.new(timeout: 10)
        wait.until { @driver.find_element(@search_box_locator).displayed? }
        search_box = @driver.find_element(@search_box_locator)
        search_box.submit
    end

    def results_text
        wait = Selenium::WebDriver::Wait.new(timeout: 10)
        wait.until { @driver.find_element(@results_locator).displayed? }
        results_area = @driver.find_element(@results_locator)
        results_area.text
    end
end
```

Then modify `./features/step_definitions/webdriver.rb`:

```ruby
require 'rspec'

Given('the homepage is opened with webdriver') do
    @simple_search = SimpleSearchPage.new(@driver, 'http://localhost:9999')
    @simple_search.open
end

When('{string} is typed into the search box with webdriver') do |value|
    @simple_search.type_search(value)
end

When('the {string} button is pressed with webdriver') do |btn|
    @simple_search.submit_search
end

Then('the results should display {string} with webdriver') do |results|
    expect(@simple_search.results_text).to eq(results)
end
```

Java

In this example, the `SimpleSearchPage` class is instantiated as needed since all state information is managed by WebDriver. To get started, create a file `./src/test/java/<Pkg Path>/pages/SimpleSearchPage.java`:

```java
import org.openqa.selenium.*;
import org.openqa.selenium.support.ui.*;

public class SimpleSearchPage {
    private WebDriver driver;
    private String url;
    private By searchBoxLocator = By.id("search_box");
    private By resultsLocator = By.id("results");

    public SimpleSearchPage(WebDriver driver, String baseUrl) {
        this.driver = driver;
        this.url = baseUrl + "/index.html";
    }

    public void open() { driver.navigate().to(url); }

    private WebElement findElement(By loc) {
        WebDriverWait wait = new WebDriverWait(driver, 10);
        return wait.until(ExpectedConditions.visibilityOfElementLocated(loc));
    }

    public void typeSearch(String query) {
        WebElement searchBox = findElement(searchBoxLocator);
        searchBox.clear();
        searchBox.sendKeys(query);
    }

    public void submitSearch() {
        findElement(searchBoxLocator).submit();
    }

    public String getResultsText() {
        return findElement(resultsLocator).getText();
    }
}
```

Then modify `./src/test/java/<Pkg Path>/WebDriverSteps.java`:

```java
import io.cucumber.java.en.*;
import static org.junit.jupiter.api.Assertions.*;

public class WebDriverSteps {
    private CustomWorld world;
    public WebDriverSteps(CustomWorld world) { this.world = world; }

    private SimpleSearchPage getSimpleSearchPage() {
        return new SimpleSearchPage(world.getDriver(), "http://localhost:9999");
    }

    @Given("the homepage is opened with webdriver")
    public void openHomepage() { getSimpleSearchPage().open(); }

    @When("{string} is typed into the search box with webdriver")
    public void theUserFillsInTheSearchBoxWith(String value) {
        getSimpleSearchPage().typeSearch(value);
    }

    @When("the {string} button is pressed with webdriver")
    public void theUserPresses(String btn) {
        getSimpleSearchPage().submitSearch();
    }

    @Then("the results should display {string} with webdriver")
    public void theUserShouldSeeInTheResults(String expectedText) {
        String results = getSimpleSearchPage().getResultsText();
        assertTrue(results.contains(expectedText));
    }
}
```

🎗️ **Pro Tip:** You can also load your Page Object models through `CustomWorld` so you don't need to instantiate them as needed.

📃 **JavaScript**

In this version of `SimpleSearchPage`, the models are instantiated in the `Before` hook so they are all available through the scenario context. To get started, modify `./features/support/webdriver.js`:

```javascript
const { Before, After } = require('@cucumber/cucumber');
const { Builder } = require('selenium-webdriver');
const SimpleSearchPage = require('../utils/SimpleSearchPage');

Before({ tags: '@webdriver' }, async function () {
    this.driver = await new Builder().forBrowser('firefox').build();
    this.pages = {
        simpleSearch: new SimpleSearchPage(this.driver, 'http://localhost:9999')
    };
});

// ...existing code...
```

Next, create a file `./features/pages/SimpleSearchPage.js`:

```js
const { By, until, Key } = require('selenium-webdriver');

class SimpleSearchPage {
    constructor(driver, baseUrl) {
        this.driver = driver;
        this.url = `${baseUrl}/index.html`;
        this.searchBoxLocator = By.id('search_box');
        this.resultsLocator = By.id('results');
    }

    async open() {
        await this.driver.get(this.url);
    }

    async typeSearch(query) {
        let searchBox = await this.driver.wait(
            until.elementLocated(this.searchBoxLocator), 10000);
        await searchBox.clear();
        await searchBox.sendKeys(query);
    }

    async submitSearch() {
        let searchBox = await this.driver.findElement(this.searchBoxLocator);
        await searchBox.sendKeys(Key.RETURN);
    }

    async results() {
        let resultsArea = await this.driver.wait(
            until.elementLocated(this.resultsLocator), 10000);
        return await resultsArea.getText();
    }
}

module.exports = SimpleSearchPage;
```

Finally, modify `./features/step_definitions/webdriver.js`:

```js
const { Given, When, Then } = require('@cucumber/cucumber');
const assert = require('assert');

Given('the homepage is opened with webdriver', async function () {
    await this.pages.simpleSearch.open();
});

When('{string} is typed into the search box with webdriver', async function (text) {
    await this.pages.simpleSearch.typeSearch(text);
});

When('the {string} button is pressed with webdriver', async function (text) {
    await this.pages.simpleSearch.submitSearch();
});

Then('the results should display {string} with webdriver', async function (text) {
    const resultsText = await this.pages.simpleSearch.getResultsText();
    assert.ok(resultsText.includes(text));
});
```

The Page Object model pattern is a useful way of organizing your UI testing
code and provides a clean abstraction for the step definitions to interact
with the UI without having to make calls directly to WebDriver.

12.4 Using Screenplay

Another software design pattern that is useful for testing user interactions against your application is the screenplay pattern. While the Page Object models we looked at in **12.3** were simple to implement directly in code, you will need a library to properly utilize the screenplay pattern.

12.4.1 Introducing the Screenplay Pattern

As the name suggests, the screenplay pattern is based on the idea of organizing your components as though your tests are a screenplay for a movie, where there are actors (your users) who are interacting with their environment (your application). In this pattern, there are five main components:

Actor Represents a person or system that interacts with your application.

Ability Allows an actor to interact with your application.

Interaction An action that an actor can perform on your application.

Question Allows you to validate the state of your application.

Task A series of interactions and/or other tasks.

For more information on screenplay, consider reading *BDD In Action, Second Edition.* It was authored by the creators of SerenityBDD and SerenityJS, which are popular tools for implementing the screenplay pattern in Java and JavaScript.

12.4.2 Using Screenplay with Cucumber

</> Example #64: The Simple Search Page Screenplay

You can test this example with the following scenario:

```
@screenplay
Scenario: the user can search with a query with screenplay
    Given the homepage is opened with screenplay
    When "something" is typed into the search box with screenplay
    And the "Search" button is pressed with screenplay
    Then the results should display "Results for: something" with screenplay
```

 **Ruby**

Screengem[145] is a gem that can implement the screenplay pattern. To get started, use the example from **12.3** and run: `gem install screengem`

---

[145]https://github.com/nulogy/screengem

This library provides base classes and mix-ins for creating **actors**, **tasks**, and **questions**, but does not have **abilities** or **interactions**.

Also, screengem persists each actor's memory globally by name. This means that you do not need to keep an instance of an actor to have access to its memory; however, you will need to clear the actors' memories before each scenario.

Since screengem does not provide an implementation for abilities, let's create one. Create a file **./feature/screenplay/abilities.rb**:

```ruby
module Abilities
    class Browser
        attr_reader :driver, :base_url

        def initialize(driver, base_url)
            @driver = driver
            @base_url = base_url
        end
    end
end
```

Tasks are a class that can execute some code. However, screengem does not have the concept of interactions. In the previous section, we implemented the **SimpleSearchPage** page object model, so let's use that as our interaction layer. Create a file **./feature/screenplay/tasks.rb**:

```ruby
require 'screengem'

module Tasks
    class OpenBrowser < Screengem::Task
        def execute
            browser = actor.recall('browser')
            page = SimpleSearchPage.new(browser.driver, browser.base_url)
            page.open
        end
    end

    class TypeSearch < Screengem::Task
        def initialize(text)
            super
            @text = text
        end

        def execute
            browser = actor.recall('browser')
            page = SimpleSearchPage.new(browser.driver, browser.base_url)
            page.type_search(@text)
        end
    end

    class SubmitSearch < Screengem::Task
        def execute
            browser = actor.recall('browser')
            page = SimpleSearchPage.new(browser.driver, browser.base_url)
            page.submit_search
        end
    end
end
```

Questions are equivalent to assertions; they help us verify the state of the environment. Create a file `./feature/screenplay/questions.rb`:

```ruby
require 'screengem'
require 'rspec'

module Questions
    class ResultsText < Screengem::Question
        def initialize(expected)
            super
            @expected = expected
        end

        def execute
            browser = actor.recall('browser')
            page = SimpleSearchPage.new(browser.driver, browser.base_url)
            expect(page.results_text).to eq(@expected)
        end
    end
end
```

Then update `./features/support/webdriver.rb`:

```ruby
# ...existing code...
Before('@screenplay') do
    Screengem::ActorMemory.instance.clear
    @actor = Class.new do
        include Screengem::Actor
        def name
            'Actor 1'
        end
    end.new
    @actor.remember(browser: Abilities::Browser.new(@driver, 'http://localhost:9999'))
end
# ...existing code...
```

Finally, create `./features/step_definitions/screenplay.rb`:

```ruby
Given('the homepage is opened with screenplay') do
    @actor.performs(Tasks::OpenBrowser.new)
end

When('{string} is typed into the search box with screenplay') do |value|
    @actor.performs(Tasks::TypeSearch.new(value))
end

When('the {string} button is pressed with screenplay') do |btn|
    @actor.performs(Tasks::SubmitSearch.new)
end

Then('the results should display {string} with screenplay') do |results|
    @actor.asks(Questions::ResultsText.new(results))
end
```

Run this example with the provided scenario, but first add the scenario tag `@webdriver` to ensure that Selenium WebDriver gets initialized properly.

▣ Java

The SerenityBDD[146] library is a popular tool for extending CucumberJVM to support page object models and screenplay. It also provides many other reporting and test support features. To get started, use the example from **11.4.2** and update your `./pom.xml`:

```xml
<dependency>
    <groupId>net.serenity-bdd</groupId>
    <artifactId>serenity-core</artifactId>
    <version>4.1.3</version>
    <scope>test</scope>
</dependency>
<dependency>
    <groupId>net.serenity-bdd</groupId>
    <artifactId>serenity-cucumber</artifactId>
    <version>4.1.3</version>
    <scope>test</scope>
</dependency>
<dependency>
    <groupId>net.serenity-bdd</groupId>
    <artifactId>serenity-screenplay</artifactId>
    <version>4.1.3</version>
    <scope>test</scope>
</dependency>
<dependency>
    <groupId>net.serenity-bdd</groupId>
    <artifactId>serenity-screenplay-webdriver</artifactId>
    <version>4.1.3</version>
    <scope>test</scope>
</dependency>
```

⚠ **Pitfall:** SerenityBDD has its own Cucumber dependency injection component, so it will cause a conflict with PicoContainer. To resolve the conflict, add the following annotation in `RunCucumberTest`:

```java
@ConfigurationParameter(key = "cucumber.object-factory",
value = "io.cucumber.picocontainer.PicoFactory")
```

Next, update the `CustomWorld` class:

```java
import net.serenitybdd.screenplay.Actor;
import net.serenitybdd.screenplay.abilities.BrowseTheWeb;

public class CustomWorld {
    private Actor actor;
    // ...existing code...

    public Actor getActor() {
        if (actor == null) {
            actor = Actor.named("user1");
            actor.can(BrowseTheWeb.with(getDriver()));
        }
        return actor;
    }
    // ...existing code...
}
```

---

[146] https://github.com/serenity-bdd

SerenityBDD ships with its own **abilities** and **tasks** for Selenium WebDriver, so we don't need to use our existing page object model. Create a file `./src/test/java/<Pkg Path>/ScreenplaySteps.java`:

```java
import io.cucumber.java.en.*;
import net.serenitybdd.screenplay.actions.*;
import net.serenitybdd.screenplay.questions.Text;
import org.openqa.selenium.By;

import static org.junit.jupiter.api.Assertions.*;

public class ScreenplaySteps {
    private CustomWorld world;

    public ScreenplaySteps(CustomWorld world) {
        this.world = world;
    }

    @Given("the homepage is opened with screenplay")
    public void theUserIsOnTheHomepage() {
        world.getActor().attemptsTo(
            Open.url("http://host.docker.internal:9999"));
    }

    @When("{string} is typed into the search box with screenplay")
    public void theUserFillsInTheSearchBoxWith(String value) {
        world.getActor().attemptsTo(
            Enter.theValue(value).into(By.id("search_box")));
    }

    @When("the {string} button is pressed with screenplay")
    public void theUserPresses(String btn) {
        world.getActor().attemptsTo(
            Click.on(By.cssSelector("input[type='submit'][value='" + btn + "']")));
    }

    @Then("the results should display {string} with screenplay")
    public void theUserShouldSeeInTheResults(String expectedText) {
        String text = world.getActor().asksFor(Text.of(By.id("results")));
        assertTrue(text.contains(expectedText));
    }
}
```

Run this example with the provided scenario.

📜 JavaScript

The SerenityJS[147] library is a popular tool for extending CucumberJS to support screenplay. To get started, use the example from **11.4.4** and run the following command:

```
npm install --save-dev \
    @serenity-js/assertions \
    @serenity-js/core \
    @serenity-js/cucumber \
    @serenity-js/playwright \
    @serenity-js/web
```

---

[147]https://serenity-js.org

Create a file `./features/support/screenplay.js`:

```javascript
const { Before, After } = require('@cucumber/cucumber');
const { actorCalled } = require('@serenity-js/core');
const { BrowseTheWebWithPlaywright } = require('@serenity-js/playwright');
const { firefox } = require('playwright');

Before({ tags: '@screenplay' }, async function() {
    this.browser = await firefox.launch();
    this.actor = actorCalled('user1')
        .whoCan(BrowseTheWebWithPlaywright.using(this.browser));
});

After({ tags: '@screenplay' }, async function() {
    if (this.browser) {
        await this.browser.close();
    }
});
```

Then create `./features/step_definitions/screenplay.js`:

```javascript
const { Given, When, Then } = require('@cucumber/cucumber');
const { Navigate, Enter, Click, Text, PageElement, By } = require('@serenity-js/web');
const { Ensure, includes } = require('@serenity-js/assertions');

Given('the homepage is opened with screenplay', function () {
    return this.actor.attemptsTo(
        Navigate.to('http://localhost:9999')
    );
});

When('{string} is typed into the search box with screenplay', function (text) {
    return this.actor.attemptsTo(
        Enter.theValue(text).into(PageElement.located(By.css('input[type="text"]')))
    );
});

When('the {string} button is pressed with screenplay', function (btn) {
    return this.actor.attemptsTo(
        Click.on(PageElement.located(By.css(`input[type="submit"][value="${btn}"]`)))
    );
});

Then('the results should display {string} with screenplay', function (expectedText) {
    return this.actor.attemptsTo(
        Ensure.that(
            Text.of(PageElement.located(By.css('div#results'))),
            includes(expectedText))
    );
});
```

Run this example with the provided scenario.

🏅 **Pro Tip:** If you are looking for a lightweight screenplay library specifically for CucumberJS, you can use `@cucumber/screenplay`.[148] To get started, run: `npm install --save-dev @cucumber/screenplay`

---

[148] https://github.com/cucumber/screenplay.js/

Afterword

The goal of this book was to introduce you to automated testing with Cucumber and provide both simple and advanced examples that you can implement in your own projects. One of my favorite programming books in the early 2010s was *Maintainable JavaScript* by Nick Zakas, which treated JavaScript as a first-class language and provided a lot of practical examples on how to implement build infrastructure for JavaScript at a time when `NodeJS` was still in its infancy. I wanted to create a similar kind of experience with Cucumber in this book, where you can read through the book once and then refer back to specific examples as you grow your experience and capabilities with the tool. I hope this book has accomplished that objective and can serve as a helpful source of information for you as you continue your automated testing journey.

Quick Pickle Recipe

Time: 🕐 15 minutes

You can use different combinations of herbs and spices for different types of pickles like bread-and-butter or dill. I personally like to use thinly sliced red onions with white vinegar and oregano, and sometimes fresh lime juice.

Ingredients:

- Cucumbers or Onions (or any vegetable)
- Herbs (thyme, dill, rosemary, oregano, etc.)
- Spices (peppercorns, celery seed, cloves, coriander, mustard, etc.)
- 1 cup vinegar (white, apple cider, depending on the flavor you want)
- 1 cup water
- 2 teaspoons salt
- 2 teaspoons sugar (optional)

Prep:

- Cut up vegetables into whatever size and shape you want.
- Place vegetables, herbs, and spices in a jar.
- Brine: mix water, vinegar, salt, and sugar in a sauce pan.

Instructions:

1) Heat the brine until boiling and then stir until all ingredients are dissolved.
2) Take brine off heat and pour it into the jar with your vegetables until they are covered.
3) Let it cool, then seal the lid tightly, and place the jar in the fridge.

You can eat your quick pickles immediately, but they will taste best after two or three days. They should keep for several weeks.

Further Reading

Smart, John. BDD in Action, 2nd Edition. Manning Publications, 2023.[149]

Shore, James. The Art of Agile Development, 2nd Edition. O'Reilly, 2021.[150]

Wynne, Matt, et al. The Cucumber Book, 2nd Edition. Pragmatic, 2017.[151]

Beyer, Betsy, et al. Site Reliability Engineering. O-Reilly, 2016.[152]

Adzic, Gojko. Specification by Example. Manning Publications, 2011.[153]

Evans, Eric. Domain-Driven Design. Addison-Wesley, 2003.[154]

Beck, Kent. Test-Driven Development. Addison-Wesley, 2002.[155]

McBreen, Pete. Software Craftsmanship. Addison-Wesley, 2001.[156]

Additional Resources

Cucumber Official Documentation: [https://cucumber.io/docs/cucumber]

Cucumber (Ruby): [https://github.com/cucumber/cucumber-ruby]

CucumberJVM (Java) : [https://github.com/cucumber/cucumber-jvm]

CucumberJS (JavaScript): [https://github.com/cucumber/cucumber-js]

Test Jam - Online Cucumber/Gherkin Editor: [https://testjam.io]

Attributions

- Cover Page Font: DejaVu Sans, DejaVu Serif
- Printed Book Font: Latin Modern Roman, Latin Modern Mono
- Cucumber Cover Graphic: Cucumber plant[157] and vines[158] by Creazilla
- Header Icons: Tabler Icons[159]
- Figure Graphics: created by Steven Hunt (unless otherwise noted)
- All graphics modifications were made using Pinta[160]

---

[149] https://www.manning.com/books/bdd-in-action-second-edition

[150] https://www.jamesshore.com/v2/books/aoad2

[151] https://cucumber.io/blog/news/the-cucumber-book-second-edition/

[152] https://sre.google/books/

[153] https://www.oreilly.com/library/view/specification-by-example/9781617290084/

[154] https://www.oreilly.com/library/view/domain-driven-design-tackling/0321125215/

[155] https://www.oreilly.com/library/view/test-driven-development/0321146530/

[156] https://www.oreilly.com/library/view/software-craftsmanship-the/0201733862

[157] https://creazilla.com/media/clipart/11988/cucumber-plant

[158] https://creazilla.com/media/clipart/11987/cucumber-plant

[159] https://icon-icons.com/pack/Tabler-icons/2518

[160] https://www.pinta-project.com

Glossary

Backend-for-Frontend (BFF) - A type of service in microservice architecture that provides endpoints for a frontend such as a web UI. It allows the UI to interact with a single service and forwards requests to the microservice(s).

Code Generator - A software tool that can automatically generate source code as part of its operation. Code generators are particularly common in the C# or .NET ecosystem with examples including the interactive form editors in Visual Studio, Entity Framework model first, and SpecFlow, which converts Gherkin feature files into C# code for the target test runner.

Dependency Injection - A design pattern in software development where the dependencies of a component are injected into it rather than it creating or managing the dependencies itself. This approach allows for loose coupling between components, making the code more modular, testable, and maintainable.

Domain-Specific Language (DSL) - A programming language designed for a specific purpose or to solve a specific set of problems, as opposed to a general-purpose language such as C++, Java, etc.

Fail Fast - A testing approach where you stop running tests as soon as a test fails instead of finishing the rest of the tests first, which provides a more rapid response (hence "fast") to CI/CD tools. The downside of this approach is that you'll lose information from any additional failures that may have occurred, so you will encounter those additional test failures one at a time in future test runs instead of all at once.

Feature - A set of functionality in your application. Example: "Customers can sign in to the online store."

Interface - In statically typed languages such as Java and C#, refers to an abstract type that acts as a contract by requiring specific methods to be present in any classes that claim to implement that type. This language feature allows for different implementations of the same interface to be interchangeable, while allowing the compiler to properly enforce types.

Microservice - A software architecture in which the service layer of your application consists of many small services that can intercommunicate. This approach is particularly useful in cloud-based applications since it allows each component of the application to scale separately based on resource demands.

Object Mapper - A library that handles serializing and deserializing data to and from objects in your programming language of choice. For example, *Jackson* can automatically convert between Java POJOs and JSON strings.

POJO - An acronym for Plain Old Java Object and refers to a Java object that represents a data model of some kind.

Queue - A messaging channel where messages are processed in First in, First out (FIFO) order. An individual message can only be received once.

Rule - A grouping of scenarios within a feature.

Scenario - A specific test example that consists of one or more steps, that can be used to validate a feature.

Scenario Outline - A set of scenarios that use the same steps, but with different parameter values. Gherkin allows for easily adding new test cases to an existing scenario outline, so you don't have to rewrite (or even worse, copy/paste!) repeating scenarios.

Singleton - A design pattern in software development in which a component exists as a single instance that can be accessed from anywhere within an application.

Step Definition - A mapping between a human-readable Gherkin step in a scenario and a piece of code that can execute the step. Steps can also contain parameters for reusability.

Topic - A messaging channel that allows messages to be published and then distributed to one or more subscribers. An individual message can be sent to multiple receivers.

Index

data table, 15, 19, 21, 53, 54, 121,
    126–129
datadog, 84
decorator, 131, 132
dependency graph, 78, 97, 98
dependency injection, 43, 124, 132,
    181, 182, 192, 197
devops, 4, 11, 78, 81, 85–87
docker, 81–84, 88, 90, 91, 139, 175,
    176, 178
docstring, 19, 21, 55, 56
dom, 157, 168
domain-specific language, 14, 15,
    197
dynatrace, 84

edge, 178
ejs, 123
end-to-end testing, 2, 8, 19, 25, 26,
    87, 115
entity framework, 13, 197
erb, 123
example, 14, 16, 20, 28, 33, 35–42,
    49, 53, 55, 59–64, 66, 68–
    70, 74, 76, 80, 88, 93, 95,
    98–100, 102, 103, 105,
    106, 109, 112, 115, 117,
    121, 124, 126, 130–133,
    137, 139, 145, 150, 156,
    158, 170, 175, 182, 183,
    185, 189
executable specifications, 10, 105
expect, 38
extension pack for java, 120

fail fast, 13, 69, 73–77, 197
failsafe, 68, 71, 143, 147
faker, 115, 116
feature file, 13, 14, 17, 20, 23, 28,
    29, 31, 32, 49, 57–59, 61–
    64, 71, 90, 99, 105, 106,
    123, 127, 130, 156, 180,
    197
firefox, 175
functional testing, 12, 25

gem, 6, 29, 45, 66, 68, 109, 140,
    141, 149, 162, 182, 183,
    189
gherkin, 1, 2, 9–11, 13–17, 19–21,
    23, 24, 27, 28, 33, 49,
    53, 55, 56, 59, 62–64, 81,
    121, 123, 127, 179, 185,
    196–198
gherkin-lint, 23
git, 18, 32, 81, 82, 87–94, 101–103,
    110
git submodule, 45, 48
github, 82, 83, 89
github actions, 18
gitlab, 18, 82, 83, 89
given, 19, 21, 22, 36
google, 178
gradle, 30
graylog, 84
groovy, 89, 97–102, 106, 123
guice, 182

handlebars, 123, 124, 126–128,
    130
hocon, 110
hook, 27, 29, 31, 32, 36, 43, 49–52,
    61, 63, 74–76, 120, 126,
    127, 129, 132, 134, 137,
    181, 187
html, 79, 105, 123, 157, 168

iframe, 157
impact mapping, 24
inedo proget, 81
injectable, 182
integration testing, 8, 9, 12, 25,
    26, 87, 149
intellij, 17, 119
interface, 72, 181, 197
interface injection, 181
ios, 169
issue tracking, 57, 60, 83

java, 3, 15–17, 29, 30, 33–41, 43,
    46, 47, 49–53, 55, 64, 67,
    68, 70, 71, 73–77, 80, 89,